THE GLORY OF VENICE

THE GLORY OF VENICE

TEXT BY DANIEL HUGUENIN
PHOTOGRAPHS BY ERICH LESSING

TERRAIL

Front cover

FRANCESCO GUARDI
Departure of the Bucintoro
c. 1766,
66 x 101 cm. (26 x 39 3/4 in.),
Oil on canvas,
Paris, Musée du Louvre.

Preceding page

VITTORE CARPACCIO
The Legend of St. Ursula.
The Departure of the Ambassadors
detail
see p. 88

Right

The Spy
Baroque period, sculpture on wood
Venice, Scuola di S. Rocco

Editors: Jean-Claude Dubost and Jean-François Gonthier
Art director: Sibylle de Fischer
English adaptation: Frances Wister Faure with Robyn Ayers
Composition: Graffic, Paris
Filmsetting: Compo Rive Gauche, Paris
Lithography: Litho Service T. Zamboni, Verona

A subsidiary of the Book Department
of Bayard Presse S.A.
ISBN: 2-87939-096-6
Printed in Italy

CONTENTS

VITTORE CARPACCIO
The Legend of St. Ursula
The Ambassadors Come
Before the King of Brittany
detail
see pp. 86-87

OVERTURE

Titian's century in itself was sufficient to express the greatness of the *Serenissima* and glorify her splendour. A single century, however, is too short a span to acknowledge the inventive genius of this city. We must peruse ten centuries of history to sum up her achievements and give her creativity its due.

The magnificence of the city does not lie solely in the perfection of her monuments, impressive though they may be, but also in her remarkable setting. Venice, built on unstable marshy islands and mudflats, was established as an urban development before 1000 AD. She soon discovered that her fragile substratum could become a springboard for the most audacious extravagances and produce spectacular results.

Torcello with its superb mosaics, Canaletto and his *vedute*, St. Mark's and the Palladian churches, the Rialto with its palaces, and the *scuole* celebrate the grandeur of Venice. From Bellini and Carpaccio to Veronese, from Giorgione and Titian to Tintoretto, from Palladio to Guardi and to Canova, an itinerary in beauty spreads out before the eye.

"The most triumphant city that I have ever seen," wrote Philippe de Commynes to the King of France in 1494. From then on, nothing would deprive Venice of her title to fame.

The Flood
detail: Rain
mosaic
Venice, Basilica di S. Marco

VENICE TRIUMPHANT

TITIAN, ARETINO, SANSOVINO

Historically, the significant turning point that raised Venice to the height of her glory came about in the middle of the sixteenth century at a moment when empires and ruling houses were quarrelling and fighting each other on the continent. This took place in a region which, until then, had been centred around the Mediterranean Sea and during a period when the world was taking on new dimensions.

The city owes much of her superb heritage to the accomplishments of a great painter who knew better than anyone how to set the scene. Titian–a legendary figure even during his lifetime–was one of many great artists that Venice delighted in producing to show herself off, confirm her solidity, and build up her prestige. Nonetheless, if Titian contributed largely to shaping the glorious imagery of Venice triumphant, he was only one of the role players on the long list of great achievers who preceded him, accompanied him, and followed him.

In 1510 when the bubonic plague–which took Giorgione's life at the age of thirty three–threatened the whole city, Venice escaped devastation by using her remarkable capacity to forge ahead blindly. This was the method she had always employed to impose her domination over her enemies and crush them. Her foes had always joined forces to curb her influence, well before she had settled on her present site along the banks

TITIAN (TIZIANO VECELLIO, C. 1485-1576)
The Assumption of the Virgin
1518, canvas, 22 x 11 ft. (690 x 360 cm)
Venice, S. Maria Gloriosa dei Frari
see pp. 34-35

Titian
Jacopo Pesaro Presented to St. Peter by Pope Alexander VI
c. 1506, canvas, 57 x 72 1/4 in.
(145 x 184 cm)
Antwerp, musée royal des Beaux-Arts

Before he was made bishop, Jacopo Pesaro (1460-1547), served with distinction as captain of a galley, fighting the Turks.

of the Rialto. Over the centuries the *Serenissima* resisted attacks by covetous barbarians, envious Frankish lords, jealous Turks, and even by the plague which had no reason to spare her more than the other cities.

Titian, a native of Pieve di Cadore in the Dolomites, son of a wealthy provincial family of high standing, was blessed with an ambitious disposition and no end of self-confidence. The years between 1510–death of Giorgione–and 1525 marked the acme of his mastery; from then on, he dominated his century, placed on a high pedestal.

After Giorgione's death, Titian followed in the footsteps of the great master who was ten years his elder. At Giorgione's side, as well as in Giovanni Bellini's studio, Titian would discover his own talent and the benefits that he could reap from it. Titian then worked for rich private collectors for whom he painted secular works. He also executed great religious scenes commissioned by churches as well as paintings for the *scuole*. The members of these religious confraternities doted upon art to provide themselves with sublime images of their opulence.

Titian, a true living myth, was treated as an equal by the Emperor Charles V. It has been said that while he was doing Charles' portrait, the Emperor picked up the paintbrush that had dropped from the artist's hands and quickly silenced the murmurs of disapproval from his entourage of courtiers with a biting: "Titian is worthy of being served by Caesar."

Would Titian have been hailed as artist of the century–like Picasso, for example, in the twentieth century–if an event independent of Venice had not helped out a little? Could it have been his exceptionally long life (it was thought for some time that Titian lived for over 100 years, although in fact he died at work on the August 27, 1576, probably at the age of eighty-eight) that earned him his title of Prince of Painters?

At the beginning of the century, art was developing and flourishing in Florence, and Rome ensured the prosperity of artists such as Michelangelo at the Sistine Chapel, and Raphael at the Vatican. The extraneous event mentioned above is the Sack of Rome which took place in 1527; this fatal blow made Venice suddenly the involuntary but willing heir to the Eternal City.

During this period, Titian–still merely a regional celebrity–became the official interpreter of the glorious hours of the *Serenissima*, succeeding Bellini in this office. Once again destiny would be in his favour.

RITRATTO DI VNO DI CA PESARO
IN VENETIA CHE FV FATTO

Hall of the Scrutino
Venice, Palazzo Ducale

This room was appointed for counting votes. Under the rich panelled ceiling, a frieze of portraits; seven were painted by Tintoretto and his pupils.

THE SACK OF ROME

On May 6, 1527, Charles V's imperial troops advanced through the vineyards covering the hillsides around the Vatican in the thick, early-morning fog. The Emperor had formed a coalition of Germans, Spanish, Alsatians, Milanese and Burgundians to punish Pope Clement VII for having joined, the previous year, the League of Cognac which had assembled the Italian cities as well as France and England against the Empire. The Pope, caught inside the besieged Vatican, survived by escaping through a secret corridor that led to the Castel Sant' Angelo. That night Rome fell into the hands of the imperial assailants. For a week, massacres, pillages and drunken riots took place. Those who could, escaped. Among them was Jacopo Tatti, called Sansovino. This architect and sculptor joined the writer Pietro Bacci, called Aretino, who had already taken refuge in Venice since the month of March. It is mainly thanks to men such as these that Venice–the last city to assume leadership in the intellectual and artistic life of Italy–would quickly take over.

After the Sack of Rome, because her government showed a less rigid attitude regarding the Counter-Reformation, Venice became a refuge for dissenters from all over Europe. The *Signoria*–the chief political council of the Republic–dared write to Charles V: "Our State and its lands are open and free to Lutherans and heretics and we cannot condemn them." At the same moment, when the Jews were being persecuted in Spain, Sansovino noted that Venice enjoyed an "extraordinary peace, as though it were the promised land."

Michelangelo was among the many 'exiles' to immigrate to Venice. Bearing the rank of Chief of Fortifications, he took asylum in Venice as he was convinced–with good reason–that the commander of the allied Florentine army was a traitor. The Council of Ten begged him to stay, offering him an annual salary of six hundred ducats and proposed to pay him whatever price he set for all the works that he could create. Michelangelo hesitated, but when he learned that the Florentine government had issued a decree stating that all known fugitives would be treated as rebels if they remained in Venice after October 7–and that his name was eighth on the list–his patriotism took precedence! He knew that a move to integrate the group of Venetian artists would be countered by his enemy Sansovino, a close friend of Aretino and Titian for the last few years. To be the second or third ranking artist in Venice when he could occupy the first place in Florence or Rome, there was no question of it! He therefore returned to Florence with the promise of an official pardon. Neither Titian nor Aretino nor, for that matter, Sansovino tried to retain him.

FRANCISCO
MAVROCENO
PELOPONNESIACO
SENATVS
ANNO MDCVIC

SHOULD ARETINO BE RE-EVALUATED?

Aretino, son of a cobbler, was born in Arezzo in 1492. In Rome at the age of twenty, he had already earned a reputation as a writer, chronicler and pamphleteer. His pasquinades–satirical lampoons against his contemporaries–were sold in loose-leaf on the street. After escaping two or three assassination attempts fomented by some of the targets of his pen, and joining up with the condottiere Giovanni de' Medici dalle Bande Nere, he came to Venice to perfect his art. Here, he put his energy to writing satirical and well-informed broadsheets with political and personal comments, approving or reprimanding the prominent personalities of his time. He enjoyed making cynical, ironic and insolent remarks, and even indulged in obscene allusions–a penchant which delighted most of his patrician friends. He also possessed qualities that they did not–these included sensitivity, fidelity, friendship, and generosity.

Aretino's portrait by Titian shows him as an imposing figure, clothed in superb silk velvet with a splendid gold chain hanging from his neck. He earned the nickname of 'the scourge of princes' and had inscribed on one of his medals: *'veritas odium paritet'* (Truth engenders Hate).

In 1530, Aretino wrote to Doge Andrea Gritti to thank him for taking him under his wing. In Venice the budding publishing business and avid public provided fertile ground for his satirical writings which were widely circulated; this success even made the venture profitable to him. Aretino became a heeded and feared commentator, able to foresee when to speak out or hold his tongue. He realised that he could manipulate public opinion with complete impunity if the *Serenissima* protected him from retaliation. At his arrival in Venice he had promised not to criticise the Council of Ten, the body that secretly handled the most important state matters.

With his friends Titian and Sansovino, Aretino led an unfettered and affluent life in his palace on the Grand Canal. Always aware of the latest goings on, he was excited by the recent artistic events and would settle himself into the middle of the incessant antagonism that he provoked and nourished. His major gift as chronicler as well as diplomat was undoubtedly his ability to convince the two monarchs who were constantly at each other's throats that he was irreplaceable. Charles V and Francis I, Emperor and King, both believed that Aretino alone formed European public opinion. The power held by the great writer, whether pleasing or annoying, was remarkable.

Aretino placed no limits on his own generosity which, however, depended entirely on the gifts that the recipients of his letters sent to placate him. His palace was as well appointed as the home of a nobleman and housed the finest art objects including paintings, sculptures and precious

TITIAN
King Francis I of France (1494-1547)
1538, canvas, 43 x 35 in. (109 x 89 cm)
Paris, musée du Louvre

Left

TITIAN
The Annunciation
c. 1565, canvas, 13 x 7 ft.
(403 x 235 cm)
Venice, S. Salvatore

Following pages

SEBASTIANO DEL PIOMBO (1485-1547)
The Judgment of Solomon
c. 1508, canvas, unfinished, 6 x 10 ft.
(208 x 315 cm)
Winborne (UK), The National Trust, Kingston Lacy

TITIAN
Venus with the Organ Player and an Amoretto
c. 1548, canvas, $58^{1}/_{4}$ x $85^{3}/_{8}$ in.
(148 x 217 cm)
Madrid, Prado

furniture, fabrics and rugs. It never emptied. Every dignitary passing through Venice wished to make his acquaintance. Nonetheless, his modest background had left him with a sincere affection for the down-and-out. All those–students, monks, priests–who had suffered an injustice came knocking at his door. He held open house and open table for unwed mothers, prisoners, jailbirds, ill-equipped soldiers, and knights-errant who sought protection. All were housed, comforted and given money. Six lovely ladies whom Venetian society immediately named 'the Aretines' ran his household.

Aretino was quite an Epicurean. He sent a note of thanks to Count Manfreddo di Collalto for having given him some hares and some thrushes: "They were so appetising that when Titian smelled their delicious aroma and saw them cooking on the spit, he took a quick peek outside where it had begun to snow, noted that the table was being set and abandoned the group of friends who had invited him out to dinner. The whole gathering unanimously bestowed rapturous compliments on the long-billed birds that were simmering with a little dried meat, two bay leaves and lots of pepper; we ate in your honour but also for our pleasure."

Aretino's most admirable gift was his capacity to promote his two closest and dearest friends, Titian and Sansovino. The deep affection that these three companions held for each other never wavered. "Titian and I were transmuted into a single person by our friendship, by honourable union and permanent will." Aretino introduced Titian to Charles V, Francis I, the Duke of Mantua, and the Duke of Urbino.

This comradly association acted as a stimulant for the writer, inciting him to exercise influence on the painter. Aretino taught Titian how to express his sentiments more freely. He urged him to adopt a far more dynamic approach to his work, to express the emotions of the flesh, and glorify the female body. From the girl shining with virginal youth (*Flora, c.* 1515, Florence, Uffizi), to the uninhibited woman happily offering her naked beauty to the evident satisfaction of an organ player, (*Venus with the Organ Player and an Amoretto, c.* 1548, Prado), what an extraordinary path the artist had travelled!

THE PAINTER'S PEN

Titian's work represented to Aretino a sort of dream awakened by brush on canvas. In a letter to the painter, he wrote: "I started to look at the admirable spectacle of the innumerable barques which were carrying as many foreigners as Venetians, all amused, not only the onlookers, but the Grand Canal itself, that entertainer of all who navigated on it. As soon as the admirable spectacle of two gondolas which had decided to make a race of it began, I took great pleasure in watching the throngs of people who had stopped to see the regatta crowd on to the Rialto bridge, on the Riva dei Camerlinghi, at the Pescheria, on the Traghetto of S. Sofia and in the Ca' da Mosto. When the crowd having joyfully applauded

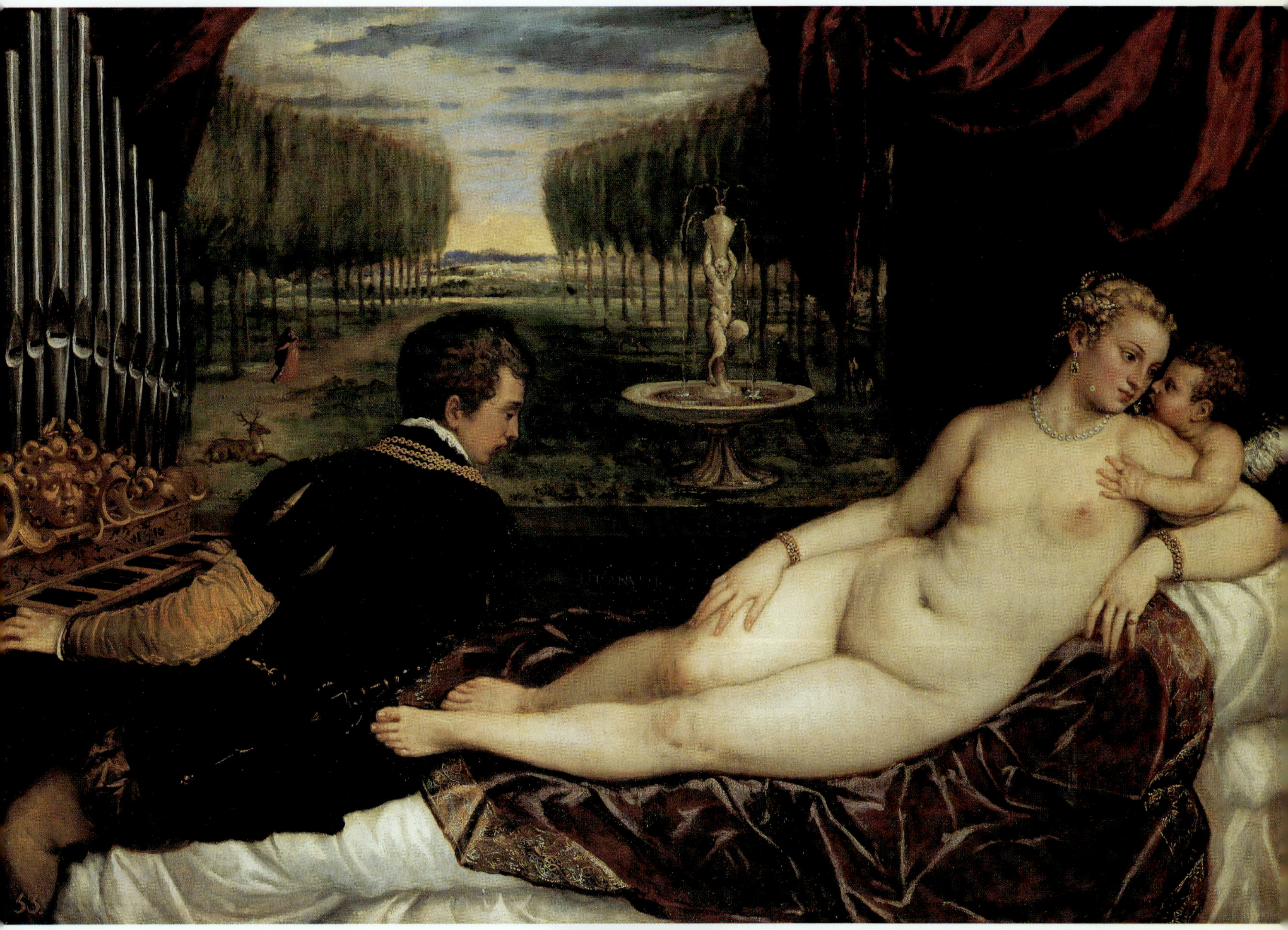

dispersed in little groups in all directions, then, like a man bored with himself who no longer knows what to do with his mind or his thoughts, I turned my eyes to the sky; never was there such a beautiful picture of shadows and light since God had made the Heavens. And it was in fact painted as those who envy you–because they cannot approach you–would like to. Admire the description that I am giving you; first the buildings, although built of real stone, seemed artificial; now imagine the atmosphere which I perceived in certain places clear and gleaming, and in other dull and livid. Imagine how I marvelled at the clouds heavy with humidity close to the roofs of the buildings, partly receding behind, and one on the right, filled with vapour, was greyish black. I was amazed by the various colours that these clouds showed. The nearest was bursting into flame like the sun and the farthest was less violently reddened. With what beautiful strokes the brushes of nature painted the atmosphere, making the palaces stand out in the same way that Titian does in the landscapes that he paints! In some places a blue-green appears, on others a green-blue, truly invented by Nature's fancy, mistress of the masters. With lights and shadows she hollowed and swelled whatever she wanted to swell and hollow; so that I, who know that your brush is the very soul of her soul, burst out three or four times with: 'Oh, Titian, where are you now?' On my honour, if you had painted what I described, you would amaze people as I was amazed; but while watching what I have described to you, I had to fill my soul with it since the splendour of a painting of this kind was not to last. In Venice (May 1544)."

Above

MARCANTONIO RAIMONDI
(ACTIVE C. 1500, D. 1534)
Aretino and the Mermaid

Left

Portrait of Pietro Aretino (1492-1556)

Right

Antonio Rizzo (c. 1435-1498)
Giants' Staircase
c. 1484
Venice, Palazzo Ducale

Named from the two gigantic statues of Mars and Neptune sculpted by Jacopo Sansovino (1566).

Then, this professed 'Condottiere of Pen and Paper' and 'Secretary of the Universe' attempted a stroke of genius. In 1547, Aretino had his letters printed, published, and circulated, hoping to win the favour of a wider public and avoid the rigorous censorship of the Church. This was in vain, however, for in 1558 all his writings were banned. The Good Fathers must have read unacceptable traces of Protestantism into Aretino's opinions and the Church had not adopted the tolerance shown by Venice's governing bodies. Even Aretino's interpretation of the Scriptures *(I Quattro Libri del'humanità di Christo)* was not enough to shield him from sanctions. Yet, remaining master of his fate, he took the precaution of dying two years before the proscription took place.

THE ARCHITECT SANSOVINO

In 1527, when Sansovino moved to Venice, he had just reached forty. He planned to spend only a few weeks there, but remained until his death forty-three years later. In 1529, after persistent recommendations by his friends Titian and Aretino, the Council of Ten placed the architect in charge of public works. It was he who devised the unique project for the Piazza S. Marco.

In 1532, Sansovino built the Palazzo Cornaro across from the old Procuratie. Four years later he adopted an architectural solution–derived in part from his experience in Rome–for a library designed to hold the Greek manuscripts offered to Venice by Petrarch and Cardinal Bessarion. It wholly transformed the centre of Venice, not only by its majestic presence, but by setting the principal buildings in a new relation to one another. He gave the Libreria Vecchia only two storeys–Doric arcades on the ground floor, Ionic columns on the first floor, and statues on a balustrade above–so that it would not be higher than the Doge's Palace nor seem too tall and narrow. Every detail played a part in the composition; the greater number of columns on the upper level balanced those of the Palace's lower loggia. The strength of the composition, the simple rhythm due to the alignment of the courses, and the matching of columns created a truly Venetian Renaissance style.

Church of S. Maria Gloriosa dei Frari
1340-1469
Venice
see pp. 34-35

At the same time Sansovino began work on a *loggetta* looking over the Piazzetta at the foot of the Campanile. He decorated this miniature triumphal arch with statues, bronze reliefs and coloured marble to contrast with the Byzantine columns and the Gothic entrance of the Doge's Palace.

His masterpiece, however, brought the worst misfortune imaginable upon the architect. Was it the fault of the labourers, or the effects of frost, or the collapse of its foundations? No one knows the answer. In any case, some of the Library's arcades collapsed in 1545 and the construction was interrupted in 1554. This mishap sent Sansovino to prison.

TITIAN
Emperor Charles V at the Battle of Muhlberg
1547, canvas 10 x 9 ft. (332 x 279 cm)
Madrid, Prado

At that time, Titian was in Augsburg working on one of the most successful paintings of his career–a portrait of Emperor Charles V on horseback at the battle of Muhlberg. It is difficult to tell in the pale light of dawn reflected by Charles V's armour as the sovereign emerges from sombre woods, whether he is leaving for battle, convinced of a favourable outcome, or if he is returning in triumph from the fray. Here, the emperor's haughtiness was outdone by the force that the artist exerted in transcribing human arrogance on canvas. Astride his black horse sporting a red harness, the emperor represents a black spectre of death against a blood red sky.

Aretino sent the hard-working Titian an account of the Sansovino affair: "Imagine how hard I cried when I realised the consequences of the catastrophe. Unable to sleep, I spent the whole night trying to measure the humiliation that such a capable and honest man has been subjected to, and I am still mulling over the cruel fate that has turned this great monument to the glory of our brother into the graveyard of his reputation. I will try not to fall into complete despair until I receive more news, for I know that the prudent Fathers of the City may take into consideration the perfect intentions of a man, rather than the professional errors of judgement that he may have committed."

To strengthen his plea, Aretino launched a campaign aimed at the patricians as well as the Doge, making the most of the incomparable talents of the architect and the difficulties that they would encounter if they had to replace him.

Sansovino was let out of jail, but forced to rebuild the Library with his own funds. This was ruinous for the architect but provided yet another opportunity for Aretino to demonstrate his legendary generosity. The writer put his entire fortune at his friend's disposal. Other citizens of the city joined forces, and Sansovino was able to pay off his debts. The flawless cohesion of these great men had once again shown its effectiveness.

TITIAN'S SOLITUDE

Only death would put an end to such solid friendships. Aretino was the first to go in 1556. Titian was only sixty-four at the time. If this death comforted those who feared the writer's pen, the painter was deeply distressed. Titian had lost not only a friend but a patron. The same summer, another illustrious sponsor, Charles V, abdicated and retired to a monastery where he died two years later. Then came the death of Sansovino in 1570. Titian found himself alone, and could only count on what energy he could still muster.

During these years, Titian protected young Veronese, who found inspiration in the creations of this great painter of princes, and he reacted in his own manner to the extraordinary bravura of Tintoretto's handling of paint and colour by adopting a more expeditious, freer, and increasingly audacious style.

Already more than eighty years old, Titian was facing a series of financial difficulties, family quarrels, and professional disputes. The dramatic events of his old age inspired his greatest creations. During the years of his mature glory, in which colour took mastery over form, he used a more limited palette of thick, phosphorescent paint, lit by shivering glimmers of light and dominated by the uneasy atmosphere of the times perceptible in all his late works. His colours darkened and his figures became less distinct and more elusive, a sign of despair and anxiety. Vasari, who came to see Titian in his studio at the time, described his canvases as "painted with large visible brushstrokes worked in patches, to such a degree that one cannot see a work close up but must stand back to take it all in." At each instant there seemed to be a danger threatening Titian's life that would brutally annihilate all that he had created. However, his painting which depicted all the most important pictorial experiences of his era dominated, unchallenged, the whole of the Venetian art world.

Two paintings from this period stand out: the *Self-Portrait* (*c.* 1550, Berlin), for which his masterly hand was still able to transcribe power and grace and *The Flaying of Marsyas* (*c.* 1570, Kromeriz). The atmosphere in

Left

LAZZARO BASTIANI (1449-1512)
Posthumous Portrait of Doge Francesco Foscari (1373-1457)
wood, $20^{1/2}$ x $16^{1/8}$ in. (52 x 41 cm)
Venice, Museo Correr

TITIAN
The Elector Johan Friedrich of Saxony (1503-1554)
c. 1550, canvas, $40^{3/4}$ x $32^{5/8}$ in. (103.5 x 83 cm)
Vienna, Kunsthistorisches Museum

TITIAN
Young Woman at her Toilet
1515, canvas, $36^{1}/2$ x 30 in.
(93 x 76 cm)
Paris, musée du Louvre

Right

TITIAN
Cardinal Pietro Bembo (1470-1547)
1545, canvas, $46^{3}/4$ x $39^{3}/8$ in.
(119 x 100 cm)
Naples, Museo di Capodimonte

the latter is particularly gloomy. The story narrates how the satyr Marsyas, proud of the tune that he is playing on his flute, defies Apollo–the god of music–to compete with him. The winner will be allowed to choose the punishment to be inflicted on the loser. The combat is too uneven for the satyr to win and he is flayed by the heartless god. Titan's genius created the most extraordinary *écorché* in the history of painting. When faced with such racking circumstances, Titian showered a bloodstained light over a world in which love no longer existed, and, from the shadows, painted the dying in a gripping representation of the fragility of man and the universe.

THE FATHER OF PAINTING

Titian gained great insight into his search for everlasting recognition in this indestructible city erected on the mudflats of a lagoon. Venice had always been threatened yet remained resplendent. In order to understand Titian's paintings, they must be placed in a historical context for they were created at a moment in time between Venice's glorious past and her uncertain future. This is where they belong.

Following the Bellini family and Giorgione, Titian reached a position that no one dared dispute. He was able to render a new vision of the world in more than just its simplicity and diversity. Carpaccio, who like Titian enjoyed the company of aristocrats and princes, manifested an elegant taste in his portrayal of noblemen and their ladies, but also painted street people, gondoliers, and beggars. In comparing the works of the two masters, it is obvious that Carpaccio caught the incident, the episode, in every one of its details–crowds in the street, on staircases, on bridges, on terraces, on the water. He was gifted with so keen an awareness and so profound a

TITIAN
The Pastoral Concert
c. 1510, canvas, 41 3/8 x 53 3/4 in.
(105 x 136.5 cm)
Paris, musée du Louvre

Attributed alternatively to Giorgione and to Titian, sometimes to both; an essential work for the understanding of the artistic climate in Venice at the beginning of the sixteenth century.

Above and right

Church of S. Maria Gloriosa dei Frari
Venice

Interior of the church for which Titian painted the *Assumption of the Virgin*.
see pp. 10 and 24

feeling for all that was Venetian that, more than any of his contemporaries, he knew how to capture the very soul of his own glorious city. With gay colours and freshness of anecdote, Carpaccio went as far as depicting the sordidness of dilapidated houses with laundry drying on a line stretched across a canal.

Titian, by reinterpreting and reconstructing reality, prepared Venice for a future which she could not have anticipated. He instigated a new assertive approach to painting, gaining freedom from the contingencies of representation and from the whims of patrons. He sought recognition through intellectual qualities, setting a new trend of European taste. Titian used every possible technical device to obtain the enigmatic lure of colour which constituted the mystery of his art. In two of his late works, light and colour seem to emerge unwillingly from the surrounding darkness, a device that gives the paintings intensity and truth. Vision and expression, therefore, became so intermingled that they could not be separated. In 1914, Elie Faure wrote: "Line has disappeared. The gradation of touches sufficiently evoke form to have it participate in the life of the whole space. Thus, continuity which makes a work alive is no longer found in the inner instinct of social solidarity seen among artists of the Middle Ages which produced invisible ties between things; continuity is no longer in the intellectual arabesque which rather speaks to the mind than stimulates the senses; it is in the mutual dependence of all the elements of the world, the forms, the lines, the colours, the air that brings them all together. Titian finished the work of Masaccio, completed that of Bellini, consecrated that of Giorgione and, before Rabelais, before Shakespeare, before Rubens, before Velázquez and Rembrandt, long before the German composers announced modern thought. He created the symphony, he was the father of painting."[1]. Titian was the first to hold true to his motto *Natura potentior ars* (Art is more powerful than Nature) and the first to liberate painting from the bondage of 'subject' and give it the autonomy that it would never relinquish again.

1. Elie Faure, *Histoire de l'art, L'Art renaissant*, 1986

PAINTING FOR ETERNITY

MOSAICS

The *Lion of St. Mark* (1516, Doge's Palace), majestic and formidable, emerges from the waters of the lagoon to take possession of the land after ruling over the seas. Vittore Carpaccio painted this emblem not only to symbolise Venice's conquest of the mainland *(terra firma)*–where she would now enjoy her accumulated wealth–but also to represent St. Mark. At the beginning of the ninth century, the city chose the Evangelist as her patron to assert proudly her independence with regard to Rome and the popes. According to a pious legend, the Saint's body was stolen from Alexandria by two Venetian sailors, Rustico di Torcello and Buono di Malamocco, who hid the holy remains in a keg of salt pork and brought them to Venice in 829 AD. A basilica was erected over St. Mark's final resting place in the heart of what was to become the City of Venice, endowing her with an almost apostolic status.

AN ADVENTURE IN CREATIVITY

When Carpaccio painted this canvas that hangs today in the Doge's Palace, he did not forget to include a grace note–'*Pax tibi Marce Evangelista meus*' ('Peace unto you, Mark my Evangelist')–to signify

Vittore Carpaccio
(active c. 1488-1526)
Doge Leonardo Loredan (1438-1521)
1501, wood, 26 3/8 x 19 1/4 in.
(67 x 49 cm)
Bergamo, Accademia Carrara

that here among the Venetian people the Saint would find rest, veneration, and honour. These words written in the book held open by the winged lion's paw, aptly symbolised both the formidable power and the pacific intentions of the Most Serene Republic.

In the background to the left is an accurate view of the Piazzetta di S. Marco seen from the Island of S. Giorgio Maggiore with the Doge's Palace, the seat of the Venetian government. To the far left is the Campanile with its restored spire and the Winged Lion again visible on the attic storey. The landscape on the right behind the lion–an allusion to Venetian domination of the seas–depicts ships under sail leaving the Arsenal on profitable voyages. Probably commissioned to decorate the walls of a

government office *(Rialto Ufficio di Camerlenghi di Comune)*, this large canvas functioned as both a heraldic figure–Lion Passant–and a historical document.

Venice abounded with many gifted painters such as Carpaccio and his colleagues who benefited from an age-old heritage of art. Born in Venice in 1465, Carpaccio seems to have spent his entire career in the city where he died in 1525. Like his friend and probable master Gentile Bellini, he was a careful observer and devoted interpreter of the realities of his era. He caught every facet of day-to-day Venice with marvellous freshness and ingenuity, becoming and remaining one of the most meticulous guides to the city.

Vittore Carpaccio
The Lion of St. Mark
1516, canvas, 4 x 12 ft. (130 x 368 cm)
Venice, Palazzo Ducale

TORCELLO, A GHOST TOWN

It is well worth making the journey to the various ghost towns scattered around the islands of the lagoon. Nowhere can you feel the meaning of Venice more intensely and understand the fascination that she holds over art lovers and dreamers of all kinds.

The island of Torcello is the most suggestive of these early settlements established in the remotest times when Venice did not yet exist. People who no longer found sufficient protection on the mainland took refuge here from the hordes of bandits and vandals swarming down from the North. Through the centuries, most of them remained fishermen and sailors, but they also adapted these inhospitable lands to their needs, creating vineyards and vegetable gardens and giving splendour to the wonderful industries of glass and lace which even today make the names of these islands famous throughout the world. Cassiodorus, a mid sixth-century witness, described the lagoons and the life of the population whose descendants later created Venice; his writings still delight historians. This Praetorian Prefect (secretary to King Theodoric of the Ostrogoths) expressed his amazement in his *Letter to the Tribunes of the Sea People who were empowered to administer Veneto*: "Here lie your houses built like sea-birds' nests, half on the sea and half on the land. Made not by Nature but created by the industry of man. For the solidity of the earth is secured only by wattle work; and yet you fear not to place so frail a barrier between yourselves and the sea. Your inhabitants have fish in abundance...."

At that time, the population of the lagoons did not hesitate to take to the sea, thus prompting Cassidorus to further remark: "It seems from far off that your barques glide on a prairie for we cannot see their hulls. They advance pulled by ropes since oars cannot be used and for fear of using the sail, your men use the slow pace of the hauliers."

This unique position described by Cassidorus must have affected the lifestyle of the inhabitants of the lagoon, the type of government that they set up, as well as their early experimentation with architecture. Life being so difficult for all (the only resources were fish and salt), Cassiodorus was prompted to write: "There is no distinction between rich and poor, the same food for all; the houses are all alike, and so envy–that vice which rules the world–is absent here. All your activity is devoted to the salt-works whence comes your wealth.... From your gain you repair your boats, which like horses, you keep tied up at your house doors."

As far as urbanisation was concerned, the towns rose from marshy wastelands and mudflats on one of the most hostile construction sites. The primitive buildings could only have existed thanks to the population's clever and practical capacity to adapt to such an environment. The entire future of the area depended on this skill. These same

wastelands that today seem so dreary, languid, and far removed from the agitation of modern civilisation housed a city, which until the tenth century represented the greatest commercial centre of the lagoon. Like Venice later on, Torcello was decked out with palaces, churches, and a grand canal. The colony flourished for some centuries. Then, when shoals and sand bars formed filling in the channel, the harbour entered into an irreparable decline and trade dwindled.

The vestiges of this age-old culture transported nineteenth-century romantic visitors into intense rapture (what James Morris called a "positive ecstasy of melancholia"). The very special aura surrounding Torcello can still be felt today.

In Venice, only two superb monuments recalling Torcello's former splendour remain today: the basilica-shaped Cathedral of S. Maria Assunta with its decor of Byzantine mosaics and the rotunda of S. Fosca with its elegant octagonal portico on three sides. It was to the East and to Byzantium that the early architects of these island towns looked for their inspiration. No matter how close the islets may be to the European mainland, they were certainly far removed from Western culture.

The vast and luminous triple nave of the Cathedral–founded in 639 AD by order of Isaac the Hexarch of Ravenna–was enlarged

and decorated with mosaics in the eleventh and twelfth centuries; it stood as a model for the later Venetian churches. Although the humble proportions of Torcello contrast with the monumentality of Venice's Basilica, the two churches have many common characteristics. If today, the first has fallen into the shadows of the second, it remains, nonetheless, the initial concept. Torcello is far more significant than just a simple model.

Torcello's church, in the same fashion as Ravenna's, kept its greatest glories inside behind an austere facade, while St. Mark's, clothed in a sheath of gold and colour, offered a magical vision outside and within. Both epitomise the eloquence of mosaics, a startling demonstration of resilience and charm. It is not by chance that a Florentine master of the Renaissance, Domenico Ghirlandaio (1449-1494), defined mosaics as "the real painting for eternity." Indeed, mosaics conserved their colour, while paintings faded over the centuries and frescoes succumbed to mould and were attacked by salt carried by the sea breezes.

Mosaics were made to endure. They consisted of a juxtaposition of pieces of stone, cubes of marble, goldleaf protected by a layer of glass paste of various colours, enamel, ceramics, and sometimes mother of pearl–always long lasting materials. These elements were set according to a pre-established design on to an *intonaco* of cement which then hardened giving extreme durability and solidity to the work produced. The Venetian craftsmen, inspired by Byzantine art, elaborated clever devices to delight the senses and seduce the eye, artfully and adroitly. They arranged the *tesserae* of the mosaics into a rich pattern of thousands of coloured dots and placed these individual elements, voluntarily or not, at a slightly different angle to the bed so that each one caught the light in a different way. The light fell in touches or caresses producing a contrived glitter; it was not simply reflected as in a mirror but refracted or dispersed in many chromatic unities.

Even as twilight deepens, a subtle play of light diffused by the mosaics illuminates Torcello's S. Maria Assunta and St. Mark's. The Torcello mosaics produce a deeper silence; at St. Mark's they burst out into song. To each edifice its vocation; to each its fate. Both monuments contribute to the glory of Venice.

ST. MARK'S

Straightway, the Basilica's fate was hinged on politics. Until 1807, S. Pietro di Castello was the Bishop's See. St. Mark's started out as a ducal chapel under the jurisdiction of the Doge and became the State Church in time. It was in this temple of civic life that the Doges were consecrated and

Above, left and preceding pages

The Flood
details
mosaic
Venice, Basilica di S. Marco

The bold representation of rain (see p. 8) and the acute realism of Noah's face, as he releases the dove from the Ark, are astounding.

ΗΑΝΑCΤΑCΙC

ΗCΤΑΥ
ΡΩCΙC

acclaimed. The Basilica served their prestige, enhanced their authority, and bore vivid testimony to their grandeur. The *Serenissima* efficiently exploited her patron saint to a political end. St. Mark not only personified the Republic, but gave licence to it.

Built to hold the remains of the Evangelist, the Basilica had never ceased to accumulate riches since its foundation in 832 AD. In Diehl's words: "For every Venetian, the upkeep and embellishment of the church was a patriotic duty in which each citizen took part with heartfelt joy, for the patron Saint was the protector of the City shielding her against all danger and saving her from all peril.... The Winged Lion, symbol of the Evangelist, reigns from the top of the column where it was placed during the thirteenth century; the City spreads out at his feet, her glorious image boasting of the Venetian conquests across the eastern Mediterranean countries. The winged-lion banner flew victoriously over the seas and floated gloriously on feast days at the top of three poles raised in front of the Basilica. All public and private life in Venice was centred around her patron saint and his sanctuary."[1]

The church's plan, as it appears from the outside, takes the form of a centralised Greek cross. Five mighty cupolas are placed at the four ends of the cross, and, in the middle where the transepts meet, a series of small windows are held up and flanked by great walled arches resembling an eastern structure. The Venetian architects had undoubtedly found inspiration in the layout of the Church of the Holy Apostles in Constantinople, as well as from oriental principles of decoration with their lavish use of multi-coloured marble and golden mosaics. It was also from the East that the most beautiful building materials came. Venetian ships sailing to the Orient were ordered to return with anything that could be used to embellish the national sanctuary. Columns, low-reliefs, statues, gold articles, in short, objects in brilliant colour were added to the already accumulated treasures. How to assemble the pieces seemed less important than the effect that would be produced on the avid eyes of the Venetians.

At the beginning of the ninth century, St. Mark's compensated for the scarcity of available land with an excess of luxury. The area, however, was progressively organised not only to improve access but to enhance the building's prestige. Unlike most other monuments which are also patchworks of the ages, St. Mark's had an unchanging singleness of intent–the glorification of Venice.

Constantinople, once master of the Orient and an ally, was pillaged of part of its treasures by the Venetians after the city's fall in 1204–a pretext that the Venetians used to organise a crusade. Among this loot, the four superb bronze horses made in imperial Rome and later sent to

Preceding pages

Basilica of St. Mark
(exterior, interior)
Venice

Left and following pages

The Treasury of St. Mark
Byzantine Art
Venice, Basilica di S. Marco

Gold and jewels in a flood...

1. C. Diehl, *La République de Venise,* 1985.

IC
XC

Constantinople, were set above the central door like a quadriga on a triumphal arch. Icons also enriched the treasures of the Basilica, and a superb group of porphyry tetrarchs (popularly known as 'The Moors') from a pre-Justinian period was chosen to adorn the angle of the tower of the Treasury.

While consolidating her position as a superpower, Venice gave herself new means to affirm her artistic independence. In 1268, a decree by the Great Council set up a school of apprenticeship to train qualified mosaicists. Several years later, the glassworks of Murano were created to provide the cubes of coloured glass necessary to clothe the Basilica. The mosaics that narrate the creation of the world date from this period as well as a story dear to the hearts of the Venetians–Noah and the Flood.

At the end of the fifteenth century, St. Mark's in its final stages shone forth like a precious and radiant 'treasure heap' as Ruskin would describe it. In the background of the *Procession on the Piazza S. Marco* (1495, Accademia), Gentile Bellini depicted the sanctuary bright with gold and light–a true model of perfection.

SANSOVINO (JACOPO TATTI, 1486-1570)
Libreria Marciana
1537-1588
Venice

The library seen from St. Mark's, with one of the four bronze horses brought back from Constantinople in 1204, and the Column of S. Todaro, one of the two monoliths erected on the Piazzetta S. Marco, also brought back from the East in the twelfth century.

THE DOGE'S PALACE

In the middle of the ninth century, during the construction of the original Basilica, when Angelo Partecipazio transferred the Doge's government to the Rialto Islands, he commissioned a ducal palace to be erected on the Piazza to serve as residence, administrative building, public archives, and Palace of Justice for the glorious and powerful *Serenissima*.

Nothing of the first edifice remains although we can assume that it was well-fortified, walled and crenellated, surrounded by a moat, and protected by corner towers according to tradition and the necessities of the times. Due to several ruinous fires over the years, but also due to its changing functions, the palace underwent a succession of transformations. Unlike St. Mark's which is Veneto-Byzantine in style, the Doge's Palace is definitely Gothic, yet the superb aspect that it has today is the work of several centuries.

It was during the second half of the fourteenth century that the new hall facing the lagoon was erected. Its unusual facade houses two loggias; the lower one displays plain Gothic arches, the other, smaller ornate lacy arcading. The walls of masonry above are cut with elegant windows and decorated with a kind of damask motif giving them a buoyant lightness. Pierced crenellations crown the top of the monument and small pinnacles adorn each corner. The final version of the Doge's Palace leaves nothing to suggest a fortress; it is a picturesque architectural structure showing off its wealth, luxury, and serenity. Even though all the frescoes and paintings were destroyed in the great fire which took place on December

20, 1577, the Doge's Palace represents the epitome of Venice's theatricality, midway between dream and reality.

BEHIND THE SCENES

Contrary to appearances, Venice is a city whose secrets are well kept. She only displays her flamboyant outer coating, guarding her secrets for those who read beyond appearances. The fragility of her substratum is well hidden from view. As early as the eleventh century, when the primitive wooden dwellings were replaced with stone constructions, the unstable soil of the mudflats had to be artificially buttressed to support them. This was accomplished by thrusting wooden stakes through the layers of sediment to form a sort of forest of props and then cleverly assembling them with wooden trellises forming subterranean platforms across which weight could be more evenly distributed, thus rendering the ground more resistant.

In the fourteenth century, the Venetians were so inspired by the campaign of embellishment of St. Mark's and the Doge's Palace that they undertook to reinforce the underpinnings of the whole city with this method. It was on this type of artificial base floating on water that houses and palaces, even more fabulous than those built on the *terra firma,* were produced by engineers and architects of great vision. Venetian architecture brilliantly demonstrates that might and splendour are often born from disadvantages overcome by audacity and inventiveness.

LUXURY, ELEGANCE, AND SERENITY

Nothing from this period equalled the magnificence of the facades of Venetian palaces. Their supreme elegance was the only excuse for the haughtiness that new money flaunted. In, 1494, when Philippe de

Commynes, sent by the King of France, discovered Venice, he was overwhelmed by the spectacle of the City:

"They took me along the *grand'rue* that they call the Grand Canal and it is quite wide (a galley can navigate through it), and I saw ships of four hundred tons and more near the houses, and it is the most beautiful street in the whole world, with the most beautiful houses and it crosses the whole city. The old houses are grand and tall, and made of good stone and painted; the others, built in the last hundred years, have facades of Istrian marble–a hundred miles from there–as well as a great amount of porphyry and serpentine at the front. Inside most of them, there are two rooms with gold ceilings, rich mantelpieces of sculpted marble, gold bedsteads, and painted and gilt screens, and lovely furniture inside. It is the most triumphant city that I have ever seen. It is a place of silk, emeralds, marbles, brocades, velvets, cloth of gold, porphyry, ivory spices, scents, apes, ebony, indigo, slaves, great galleons, Jews, mosaics, shining domes, rubies and all the gorgeous commodities of Arabia, China and the Indies. Venice is a treasure-box."

Like St. Mark's, a Venetian palace bedazzles the eye not only with the exterior beauty of its facade but also with the charm of its interior. The luxury of the facades rivals that of the courtyards, often with an outside staircase and a sculpted wellhead. Open-work loggias are found everywhere; through the dainty arcades of the columns, the view spreads forth over water.

Venetian domestic architecture followed coherent rules that were both artistic and functional. Each floor fulfilled a specific function: stores on the porticoed ground floor *(piano terra);* offices on the mezzanine *(mesà)*; living quarters and reception room *(salone)* on the main floor *(piano signorile)*. In the well-lit houses, rooms were set on each side of a central hall *(portego)* in order to provide natural ventilation which helped reduce the summer heat and fight dampness. The bedroom of St. Ursula and the *studiolo* of St. Augustine as depicted by Carpaccio caught the very special intimacy of Venetian apartments, with their discrete elegance and their beauty that invites contemplation.

Left

Vittore Carpaccio
Doge Leonardo Loredan
detail of the clothing

Below

The Doge's *corno*
Venice, Museo Correr

Following pages

Gentile Bellini (1429-1507)
Procession of the Relic of the True Cross in the Piazza S. Marco
1496, canvas, 12 x 24 ft. (367 x 745 cm)
Venice, Accademia

SAILORS AND MERCHANTS

CONSTANTINOPLE, MARCO POLO, THE ARSENAL

The resources that Venice could not find on her small plot of land with its fragile substratum, she had to seek elsewhere. She had already enlarged her boundaries to the utmost. Her population which "neither labours nor sows nor harvests," as described by a sixteenth-century traveller, fought for its possessions on the seas and the oceans in the same manner that other peoples went to war on the *terra firma.*

Venice deliberately chose a maritime existence to escape from her own inadequacies. She erected vast warehouses away from covetous eyes and constructed well-protected dockyards for her active shipbuilding industry. At a very early date, this seafaring population produced merchants, traders, and a navy that crushed–with force or by cunning–many of the Levantine territories able to provide the goods that could not be produced on such inadequate landholdings. This aggressiveness was fundamental in securing the wealth and the greatness of Venice for centuries and provided regular access by the sea to the points at which near-eastern merchandise could transit through a protected trade corridor.

THE COLONIAL EMPIRE

Venice's colonial empire was set up in 1204. In April 1201, the Republic promised powerful assistance to Pope Innocent III's

Domenico Tintoretto (1560-1635)
The Conquest of Constantinople in 1204
Venice, Palazzo Ducale, Maggior Consiglio

Fourth Crusade against the Sultan of Egypt, by supplying and transporting the Frankish troops to the Holy Land. To further strengthen Venice's unshakeable commitment to Christianity, Doge Enrico Dandolo and some of the Frankish barons made a secret agreement, that, instead of proceeding directly to Egypt, the expedition would first go to Constantinople to put the young emperor Alessio back on his throne. Once back in power Alessio would be able to serve the Christian undertaking. When several of the barons were forced to desist because they lacked the means to meet the expenses agreed upon, Dandolo took over the crusade and re-routed the army to Zara, a city in Hungary which the Venetians wanted to take back from the Turks. The battle of Zara (1202) was a just a rehearsal for the future storming of Constantinople. Thanks to the shrewdness of Dandolo, Venice made a huge profit from these expeditions. Domenico Tintoretto, the second son of Jacopo Robusti Tintoretto the elder, painted a grandiose interpretation of the event. The new Latin Empire of Constantinople was established. Dandolo's foresight provided enormous wealth since three quarters of the booty was attributed to Venice as well as privileged trade agreements between the Republic and the former Greek hegemony. "After Constantinople finally fell (April 12, 1204), for the next several days the Venetians intelligently took their pick of the relics and precious objects with which Constantinople overflowed. Today St. Mark's treasury testifies to the Venetians' sure and efficient methods of plundering and to their absence of scruples, in spite of the fire that destroyed a good part of this loot in 1231."[1]

Domenico Tintoretto
The Turks Surrender at Zara, the Citizens Hand over the Keys
detail
Venice, Palazzo Ducale, Maggior Consiglio

Christianity's domination over the East did not last however, because the Genoese joined the Byzantines to help them recover their capital in 1261. Paradoxically, it was the Mongols who, having crossed the Carpathian Mountains and having arrived on the outskirts of Vienna in 1241, would give hope to Venice. The Mongols, both monotheists and tolerant of Christianity, must have appeared as possible allies against Islam. In any case this was how Venice decided to consider them.

THE GLORIOUS ADVENTURE OF MARCO POLO

Marco Polo's exploits as recorded in his *Livre des Merveilles* were food for imagination. His adventures were made possible by the reopening of routes to the Far East after the alliance with the Mongols. The routes that Marco Polo opened would never close again, to such an extent that E. Power remarked that: "Alive in the thirteenth century, [he] discovered China; dead in the fifteenth century, he discovered America."

Marco Polo's personality exemplified many of the characteristics of his motherland, such as an extreme curiosity for all novelty and a decided preoccupation with commercial interests. Easily

1. C. Diehl, *op. cit.*

adaptable, tolerant by conviction as well as out of self interest, always stimulating the ambitions of his fellow citizens, Polo combined all the best qualities of a doge, qualities that would procure the glory of Venice. Undoubtedly, he would have been worthy of a commemorative statue at another moment in history, but at the beginning of the fourteenth century a monument like the beautiful marble of Antonio Venier by the young sculptor Jacobello della Masegne (1383-1409) was reserved only for the Doge.

The Polos–Marco, his father and uncle–were not the first foreigners to travel to Asia, but it appears that they were the first Westerners to travel into the heart of China. More interesting, however, is the fact that Marco Polo was the first visitor to record and publish his observations. After a twenty-four year stay in the Far East (between 1271 and 1295) where he escaped many treacherous situations, Marco Polo was imprisoned in Genoa in 1298 following one of the small wars that were regularly fought between the Venetians and the Genoese. His captivity was a godsend for posterity. Condemned to inaction, Marco Polo spent his incarceration dictating his memoirs to a companion in exile by the name of Rustichello, from the town of Pisa. All this material transcribed in Old French–the colloquial language of the merchants of the time–must have impressed the Venetians, since his memoirs were rapidly translated into Latin and Italian.

After his liberation, Polo went over the notes taken down by his scribe and took great care to be sure that the journal was circulated among his contemporaries. All this took place long before the invention of the printing press.

Ducal Commission
1508, illustrated manuscript
Venice, Museo Correr

Instructions given by Doge Leonardo Loredan to Captain Giovanni Mauro, assigning him to different Eastern ports to load cargoes of spices.

Following pages

Logbook of a Venetian Galley
with a compass on the metal binding
Venice, Museo Correr

FROM IMAGINATION TO REALITY

Marco Polo was forced to overcome much scepticism from the public. Nonetheless, the descriptions of daily life of the populations that he came in contact with during his travels are extraordinarily precise. The clothing, the food and the sexual, funerary, and religious customs were reported with such simplicity and pertinence that they still enthral today's reader. Whether he narrated imaginary adventures inspired by allegoric fables of unknown mythologies is a matter of conjecture, but the tales with which he held his readers and listeners spellbound were based on real observations.

A combination of luxury and comfort, this was the fanciful world that Marco Polo made of all that he discovered and that he found difficult not to compare with Venice. His descriptions of China's imperial palaces were enough to make any Venetian jealous and this was undoubtedly what he had set out to do. His accounts of the summer capital of the Kublai Khan surpassed even his contemporaries' wildest dreams of

luxury. He was delighted to discover that the sovereign had the choice of two palaces, one built out of marble, the other made of bamboo that could be dismantled.

The patricians of Venice found Polo's revelations all the more difficult to swallow because of their ring of truth. His tales troubled their deep-seated feelings of superiority and caused them to speculate whether or not marvels surpassing those of Venice could exist somewhere else in the world.

Marco Polo was a man of his era–the thirteenth century–imbued with his own beliefs and legends. His point of view resembled not only that of an anthropologist, but also that of a businessman who never missed making a profit when it came his way. From the steps of Asia Minor to the heart of China, through Mongolia and Siam, Japan, Sumatra, Ceylon, India and Persia, everywhere he travelled, the insatiable discoverer jotted down details about agricultural and industrial production and the conditions of trade.

Furthermore, when travelling through India on the way back to his native city, he could not keep from describing the galleys on which the merchants came and went, with the same meticulousness that he applied to all his observations. Without pretending to have the competence of a naval architect, he planned to give useful advice to those in Venice who were in charge of building the vessels that transported goods or went off to battle. Here is what he said with regard to the boats that he crossed in the Indian Ocean:

"Some ships, in particular the largest, have thirteen compartments inside them made of strong well-assembled boards; thus, if the hull be pierced somewhere by hitting a rock or that a whale runs into it while searching for food, then the water enters the opening and fills the hold that is never been filled with anything; the seamen look for the compartment that is taking in water and empty it into the others, for the water can not flow from to one another, so watertight are the compartments; they then repair the ship and put back the merchandise that they had taken out."

Not only is this passage significant of Marco Polo's approach, but it also reflects something typically Venetian. Like his compatriots, whether merchants, politicians, craftsmen, or artists who had adapted to empirical ways of thinking, he believed that nothing should ever be taken for granted; he observed, then interpreted. Consciously or not, Venetians have wanted their achievements to last forever, but they well knew that reaching immortality could only be accomplished through constant research and innovation. Such an attitude was, of course, shared by artists.

Tomaso da Modena (1325-1379)
Triptych of the Virgin Holding the Divine Child, with Doge and King
Tempera on gilded wood,
31 1/8 x 21 1/4 in. (79 x 54 cm)
Karlstejn (Czech Republic)

Right

L'Aliense
(Antonio Vasilacchi, 1556-1629)
Baldwin of Flanders, Crowned Emperor of Constantinople in 1204
Venice, Palazzo Ducale

Preceding pages

Cosme Tura (c. 1430-1495)
Angels Holding Christ's Body
c. 1475, wood, 17 1/2 x 33 3/4 in.
(44.5 x 86 cm)
Vienna, Kunsthistorisches Museum

FROM WOOD TO CANVAS

Venice became a laboratory of permanent experimentation for painting as well as architecture. Talented artists from other cities came to exercise their profession in Venice and liberated themselves from their previous habits and techniques. Tommaso da Modena (1325-1379), one of these immigrant artists, used the radiance of gold to symbolise eternity in his *Triptych of the Virgin Holding the Divine Child, with Doge and King* (Karlstejn). Neither the Virgin, nor those who accompany her could have been portrayed in a less sumptuous decor. Gold was not only significant for its power to suggest richness and splendour but also for its resistance to tarnishing and its adaptability. It was certainly the substance that best suited the magnificence of Venice, and more than any other, it had the opacity to hide the wood which artists used as a support for painting at the time.

It was not until the fifteenth century that Venetian artists freed themselves from wood panel. Before then, cloth had only been used by artists for ephemeral needs such as processional banners. Woven fabric was manufactured in great quantity and readily available from one of the most highly developed enterprises of this seafaring population–the sailmaking industry. Artists began to supply themselves with this revolutionary material for their painting. Canvas gradually became a support for permanent works of art around 1450 in the circle of painters around Mantegna and the Bellini. It was cheaper, lighter and more portable than wood; it only needed to be removed from its stretcher, or taken apart at the seams (if size required) and rolled up with care. Thus, paintings acquired a greater autonomy, for they could be transported rapidly throughout the whole of Europe.

GIOVANNI BELLINI (1430-1516)
Enthroned Virgin and Child, with Saints Peter, Catherine, Lucy, and Jerome, while an Angel Plays the Viol
1506, altarpiece
Venice, S. Zaccaria

The gentle gesture of the Virgin's cupped hand cradling the foot of the Christ Child has fascinated many commentators.

JACOBELLO DELLA MASEGNE (1383-1409)
Doge Mocenigo
Venice, Museo Correr

Right

FOLLOWER OF GENTILE BELLINI
Audience of an Ambassador in an Eastern City
detail
first half of the sixteenth century, canvas, 68 7/8 x 79 1/8 in. (175 x 201 cm)
Paris, musée du Louvre

Some, however, continued to paint frescoes in churches, like for example Pisanello (1395-1450) with his extraordinary *St. George* (Verona), which can be compared to the superb paintings of Paolo Uccello. Later, Cosmè Tura (1430-1495), an artist influenced by Mantegna's sculptural style combining rock effects and intricacy of details, continued to work exclusively on wood *(Angels Holding Christ's Body, c.* 1475, Vienna), whereas Antonello da Messina (1430-1479), having studied the northern masters with passion, transposed the new Flemish oil technique from wood to canvas when he painted his *St. Sebastian* (Dresden) in Venice or his famous *Portrait of a Condottiere* (1475, Louvre).

This change of support brought about a progressive transformation of the methods of painting. The great Venetian masters adapted the oil-on-canvas technique to their particular needs; it was they who first exploited systematically the differences in texture of the canvas and experimented with the thickness of the paint. Carpaccio and Giorgione exemplify the variations in practice of individual painters; the first applied paint in thin layers, while the latter used a more loaded brush to produce the thickness of pigment that would become characteristic of Venetian painting in the sixteenth century.

Right

The Venetian Fleet Led by Admiral Francesco Morosini
seventeenth century
Venice, Museo Correr

Thanks to his great victories over the Turks, Morosini became doge in 1688.

Below

Chart of the Meridians
Baroque period, ivory column
Venice, Museo Correr

SEGVISCE L.ARMATA TVRCA, CHE FVGGE SEBENE PIV̀
A, ARRIVA DVE DELLE PIV̀ GROSSE GALERE, E LE
APRILE 1659.

Right

Lamp from a Turkish Galley
bronze
Venice, Arsenale, Naval Museum

Two Venetian Quivers with Arrows
seventeenth century, gilded wood
Venice, Arsenale, Naval Museum

REAR BASE: THE ARSENAL

Venice housed the greatest shipyard of the Western World, her largest industrial establishment. The Arsenal, originally built in 1104 on two adjoining islets in the lagoon, was continually expanded and refurbished during the fourteenth century and for the following two hundred years. It never ceased to increase its productivity, nor did its naval architects fail to put their talent to good use. It was from the yards of this huge complex that Venice's mighty war fleet and merchant navy set out to sea to become the major instrument of the Republic's commercial and political ascendancy.

In 1423, in his famous speech on the state of the Republic, Doge Tomaso Mocenigo made an inventory of 3,000 merchant vessels and 300 war galleys. Of the 190,000 inhabitants of the lagoon, 17,000 worked at the Arsenal, and the navy engaged 25,000 seamen. Without the Arsenal, Venetian merchants, in spite of their cleverness, would not have been able to build up or hold a dominant position in the Mediterranean.

The austere architecture of the Arsenal, a true fortress with high protective walls and square towers, contrasts with the splendour of the palaces. Nowhere is there a decorative touch. The only departure from total starkness is Sansovino's low relief above the entrance. The Arsenal in itself was overwhelming–it attested to the power of the State. For it was the State that determined the number of vessels to be built, maintained, armed, appointed the captains, and decided which merchandise to transport. A detailed calendar of convoy movement provided an efficient rotation of the galleys.

Inside the Arsenal working methods were strictly enforced. Authority was in the hands of the foreman *(proto)* who applied techniques that had come down to him from his forebears. Disregarding all theoretical considerations, the shipwright had no knowledge of either Euclid's geometry or fluid mechanics; his skill, which resided so much in his eye, was based on experience and on his ability to set correct measurements. This was the kind of practice that made Venice's art of shipbuilding so difficult to imitate and even more difficult to outdo; for, as always, she resorted to an empiricism typical of her genius. The Arsenal confirms that Venice's true might was born from an unshakeable self-confidence.

Dante, who certainly visited Venice on many occasions, for the last time as Ambassador from Ravenna, discovered the Arsenal at a time when it was probably at its maximum activity. The following passage from Dante's Inferno (Canto XXI), translated by Longfellow, demonstrates his theological and dramatic vision of the human condition:

As in the Arsenal of the Venetians
Boils in the winter the tenacious pitch

To smear their unsound vessels ov'er again,
For sail they cannot; and instead thereof
One makes his vessel new, and one recaulks
The ribs of that which many a voyage has made;
One hammers at the prow, one at the stern,
This one makes oars and that one cordage twists
Another mends the mainsail and the mizzen.

This description of the assembly lines where thousands of men were busily building the ships that would soon leave the drydocks ready to transport merchandise or defend the Republic, conveyed a bleak picture of working conditions. This was the hidden face of the glory of Venice. The city only revealed what she chose. The Arsenal evinced curiosity. Dante was probably not aware that the Republic highly valued and took great care of this type of craftsman. Venice knew that her success rested on the quality of their work. "...from the fourteenth century on there

ERHARD REUWICH
View of the Doge's Palace and St. Mark's from the Canal
1486, woodcut printed in Mainz
Venice, Libreria Marciana

Erhard Reuwich
Construction of a Galley at the Arsenal
1486, woodcut printed in Mainz
Venice, Libreria Marciana

Signboard for a Workshop at the Arsenal
Sixteenth century, painted wood
Venice, Museo Correr

was not a Venetian who did not own something; and every man was able to find a paid job. There was no proletariat; social crises were unknown."[1]

The beautiful series of woodcuts that relate the pilgrimage of Bishop Breidenbach in the fifteenth century depict one of the last phases of construction of a Venetian galley. There is nothing Dantesque in this rendition by the engraver Reeuwich. In the same series, another scene shows the Piazza S. Marco before the terrible earthquake that destroyed the Campanile.

THE BUCINTORO

The great Venetian holiday centred around an elaborate vessel is said to have begun in 998 AD to commemorate the victory over the Slavs of Istria and Dalmatia. The name *Bucintoro* given to this extraordinary barge may be derived from *ducentorum hominium*, that is, the two hundred men who rowed it, or from *buso*, the Venetian word for boat with the suffix *oro* (gold). The *Bucintoro*, sumptuously gilded and carved, was used to take the Doge with his Signoria out to the Lido to perform the Marriage with the Sea every Ascension day. Clothed in his most lavish purple and gold attire, the Doge would throw a gold ring into the water while pronouncing the ritual formula: "We espouse thee, O Sea, in a token of perpetual sovereignty." Then after celebrating a Mass, a gigantic banquet was held at the palace, and games and dances took place throughout the city.

A Frenchman, Joachim du Bellay, stopping in Venice on his way back from Rome, took pleasure in making fun of this symbolic act. Included in *Les Regrets* (1558) is a sarcastic description of the ceremony:

It's fun to see, Magny, these magnificent gudgeons,
Their superb Arsenal, their vessels, their shores,
Their Saint Mark, their Palaces, their Rialto, their port,
Their cambio, their profits, their banks and their traffic,
But what deserves a closer look,
Is that these old cuckolds have wed the sea
They are the husbands, and the Turks the adulterers.

There may be a hint of envy in the poet's words and also some regrets for not having found the likes of Venice elsewhere, but there is also a premonition hidden beneath the sarcasm; for the battle of Lepanto, with the mock victory of the Venetian 'husband' over the Turkish 'lover' would take place. In 1571, the Venetians and the Turks went to war once more.

1. C. Diehl, *op. cit.*

INTO THE RENAISSANCE

BELLINI AND CARPACCIO

L'ALIENSE (Antonio Vasilacchi)
Catarina Cornaro, Widow of the King of Cyprus, Disembarks in Venice
detail
c. 1500, canvas, 7½ x 23 ft.
(229 x 707 cm)
Venice, Museo Correr

In the last days of the Middle Ages, Venice seemed in advance of her time, already living a renaissance. She stayed away from the quarrels still raging between other cities on the *terra firma* and maintained a balance between ambitions and achievements, between riches and customs, between hope and virtue. In 1364 Petrarch praised the Republic as:

"...the one home today of liberty, peace and justice, the one refuge of honourable men.... Venice, rich in fame, mighty in her resources but mightier in virtue, solidly built on marble but standing more solid on a foundation of civic concord, ringed with salt waters but more secure with the salt of good counsel."

RIALTO AND SAN LORENZO: WOOD AND STONE

Towards the end of the fifteenth century, Venetian painting combined a faithful interpretation of reality with a convincing rendition of the fancies of the period. The buildings along the canals were depicted in minute detail and the population was shown taking part in the civic as well as religious festivities–privileged moments for the community to reassert its identity.

Vittore Carpaccio was thirty years old when he painted *The Miracle of the Cross at the Rialto* (*c.* 1494, Accademia). The scene describes the Grand Canal with great topographical precision. Many of the architectural details are still visible today: the Gothic windows, the church towers, the chimneys shaped like up side down bells so characteristic of Venice. The Rialto bridge was still in wood with a central drawbridge system which allowed galleys to pass through to unload their precious goods in the warehouses–*fondachi*–along the Grand Canal. After the original bridge collapsed in 1527, it was restored again in wood, but in 1591 it was entirely replaced by the stone one that is still there today.

A painting by Gentile Bellini depicts the celebration of another miracle: *The Miracle of the Cross at S. Lorenzo Bridge* (1500, Accademia). The modest bridge over the canal built of bricks and stone which, if we believe the artist, was probably the first of its kind at the end of the fifteenth century. The painting shows the moment when Andrea Vendramin, leader of the Brotherhood of St. John the Evangelist, recovered the relics of the Holy Cross that had fallen into the canal during a procession while the fascinated crowds lined the quays, watching the miracle take place. When religious stories are so closely tied to everyday life, hell and damnation are held at bay.

Right

Gentile Bellini
Miracle of the Cross at S. Lorenzo Bridge
1496, canvas, 11 x 14 ft. (323 x 430 cm)
Venice, Accademia

Andrea Vendramin, leader of the Brotherhood of St. John the Evangelist, recovers the relics of the Holy Cross that had fallen into the S. Lorenzo canal during a procession.

THE SCUOLE: WELL-ORGANISED CHARITIES

In Venice from the beginning of the fourteenth century, economic and commercial activities were organised into lay confraternities called *scuole*. Most of the members worked as craftsmen such as cobblers, tanners, stonecutters, etc. often formed into groups with a common ethnic background such as Slavic, Macedonian, or Albanian. These associations were assigned a ceremonial role and carried out devotional practices as well as charitable activities. The Venetian government relied upon some of them to distribute public funds. Their particular kind of service directed at assisting the needy helped prevent movements of unrest from developing in the poorest classes of society. The Venetian confraternities oftentimes owned their establishment and practised a lay piety somewhat independent from ecclesiastical authority. Several *scuole* acquired a higher renown thanks to the talent of the artisans and painters who were called upon to decorate their premises, for example, the Scuola di S. Rocco with the works of Tintoretto in the second half of the sixteenth century.

Earlier, between 1490 and 1498, Carpaccio painted scenes celebrating the legend of St. Ursula for a confraternity bearing her name. These works, that once decorated the oratory of the ancient Scuola di S. Orsola, served not only as a pretext to evoke the major moments in the life of the Saint, but transposed the legend into reality with great freedom. While Gentile Bellini adopted a detailed documentary approach, Carpaccio created a "magical synthesis between the abstraction of perspective and a rational vision of reality."[1]

1. Terisio Pignatti, *L'art vénitien*, 1992.

Amateurs of Flemish painting have admired the reliquary painted by Hans Memling for St. John's Hospital in Bruges (1489), one of the many and one of the most beautiful pictorial versions of the life of St. Ursula–a popular subject at the end of the Middle Ages. The romantic and poetical incidents in the life of the Saint were narrated in the *Golden Legend* by the thirteenth-century writer Jacobus de Voragine, Bishop of Genoa. A version of these tales, from which Carpaccio must have found the subject matter for his paintings, was printed in Venice in a 1475 translation signed by Niccolò Malerbi from a French edition by Nicolas Jenson.

THE LEGEND OF ST. URSULA

Once upon a time, a Christian princess was born in Brittany. She was wrapped in furs, hence her name Ursula which means 'little bear.' The story tells how Ursula accepted the hand of the King of England's son, Hereus, on the condition that he first receive a Christian baptism and then wait three years before marrying her–time for her to make a pilgrimage to Rome. She insisted upon being escorted by ten virgins and each one of these being accompanied by a thousand others. The prince, charmed by Ursula's beauty and wisdom, agreed to her terms. The pilgrims reached Rome without mishap, but when, on their way back to England accompanied by the Pope and his retinue of cardinals, they arrived in Cologne, the city was under siege by the Huns. Ursula's followers were massacred. When she refused to marry the son of the King of the Huns, she was shot down by three arrows.

Carpaccio's important series of paintings demonstrates all his qualities as a charming and fanciful narrator and interpreter of the life of Venice. While respecting the general themes of the legend, the artist greatly enriched their meaning. This tale gave birth to passionate love stories, alive with voyages to far-off countries, pageantry, courtiers, seascapes, and marine architecture.

Although the chronology in the series of paintings does not quite follow the events of the legend, Carpaccio devised a subtle narrative progression, constructing space around each episode. *The Ambassadors Come Before The King of Brittany* depicts envoys coming and going before the King to propose and arrange the union of Princess Ursula and Prince Hereus. Groups of noblemen in elegant clothing–inspired by the many embassies in Venice–are witnessing the different negotiations taking place under Venetian porticoes. The lagoon criss-crossed by sailboats, the costumes of the onlookers, and the architecture of the palaces are characteristic of the artist's descriptive style. All of these scenes take place in the Venice of the painter's time–a poetic licence. The atmosphere reflects the dignified nonchalance that Venetians put on when performing the most solemn acts;

Above, left, and following pages

Vittore Carpaccio
The Legend of St. Ursula
The Departure of the Engaged Couple
details
canvas, 9 x 20 ft. (280 x 611 cm)
Venice, Accademia
see p. 204

VICTORIS
CARPATIO
VENETI·
·OPVS·
MCCCCLXXXXV·

VITTORE CARPACCIO
The Legend of St. Ursula
The Ambassadors Come Before the King of Brittany
details
canvas, 9 x 19 ft. (275 x 589 cm)
Venice, Accademia

VITTORE CARPACCIO
The Legend of St. Ursula
The Departure of the Ambassadors
canvas, 9 x 8 ft. (280 x 253 cm)
Venice, Accademia

Right

The Legend of St. Ursula
The Return of the Ambassadors to England
canvas, 9½ x 17 ft. (294 x 527 cm)
Venice, Accademia

Following pages

Left
The Legend of St. Ursula
Meeting with Pope Cyriac in Rome
canvas, 9 x 10 ft. (281 x 307 cm)
Venice, Accademia

Right
The Legend of St. Ursula
The Dream
canvas, 9 x 8½ ft. (274 x 267 cm)
Venice, Accademia

their taste for sumptuousness is expressed by the splendor of the decor with its lavish encrustation of coloured marble.

However there are several exotic touches in the *Return of the Ambassadors:* the non-Venetian architecture of the royal palace with its unadorned triumphal arch, the marble reliefs on the walls and the nude statue on the roof. All these details seem in complete contrast with the most typically Venetian of bridges. Moreover, the man with the fur hat standing in the foreground with his back to the viewer might be described as typically English.

The scene of St. Ursula's departure (often called *The Departure of the Engaged Couple*) is both the largest painting in the series and displays the greatest scenographic complexity. This canvas assembles several different episodes. On the left, behind Hereus, who is in England taking leave of his parents, is a large vessel sailing off before the wind; written backwards on the sail is the word *malo*–a deadly omen announcing that there will be no return. In the middle of the canvas, the scene is taking place in Brittany where the Prince disembarks and meets his fiancée for the first time. On the right, her parents are bidding farewell to the couple. In the background, the young people and their party are boarding vessels for the pilgrimage to Rome.

The tale continues, for it is during the crossing that Ursula has a premonition revealing her fatal destiny–*Ursula's Dream*. An angel announces to her that on the return journey she will be made a martyr on account of her adherence to the Christian faith. The message is made clear by the palm leaf held in the angel's right hand.

In the first light of dawn, Ursula sleeps on a bed with no surrounding curtains, her slippers neatly arranged on the carpet; a gold crown–which is one of her attributes–lies at the foot of the bed. The door of the room is wide open and beyond, another opening creates a skilful lighting effect. The mullion of the window is half-hidden by one of the bedposts holding up the canopy. On the sill beneath the leaded window panes, a bouquet of carnations sits in a wide-necked vase–a symbol of the promised wedding–*ratum sed non consummatum*. The other half of the window is entirely overrun by myrtle (this plant symbolized love and was dedicated to Venus) growing out of narrow-necked vase; the myrtle speaks of love and death in the silence of dreams. The long hollow made by the bedclothes draws attention to the husband that was never to be, and the bedposts holding up the canopy evoke the final painting where St. Ursula's body lies in state on an ornamental bier.

The Saint's room describes to perfection the interior of a Venetian palace at the end of the fifteenth century. John Ruskin wrote his sincere admiration for the work: "...everything is chaste and virginal and executed with loving care, the angelic vision appears to the peacefully sleeping Saint to bring her the palm of martyrdom."

The episode of the angel's tragic tidings is followed by the meeting with the Pope in Rome. After the pilgrims' safe arrival, attested to by the long cortège proceeding up from the port in the distance, the engaged couple meet with Pope Cyriac outside the city walls in front of the great mass of Castel Sant' Angelo. For the first time in the series, neither the landscape nor the postures of the Pope's retinue are Venetian.

In the *Meeting with Pope Cyriac in Rome,* the circular form of the imposing pontifical castle that dominates the picture curls into an elegant spiral of virgins and dignitaries of the Church in procession. Executed in 1494–at the same time as the *Miracle of the Relic of the True Cross*–this painting displays all the subtleties and the charm that so enthralled Venetian art lovers during the calm days of the Renaissance.

Accompanied by the Pope and his cardinals, Ursula sails on the Rhine. *The Arrival at Cologne,* shows the party entering the city which is under siege by the Huns. In the next picture *(Martyrdom of the Christians under Cologne and the Burial of St. Ursula)* the left-hand scene depicts the Huns, who have just taken the city, massacring the pilgrims and the Pope. While the Saint kneels waiting to be struck by arrows, a warrior–the son of the King of the Huns–gazes at her, moved and enamoured. On the right Ursula, the martyr, lies on her bier carried on the shoulders of four bishops followed by a cortège of prelates and the faithful. Doubtless, portrayed among the mourners were officials of the Scuola di S. Orsola who commissioned Carpaccio's series of paintings.

Thanks to the pious legend of St. Ursula and seized by a natural leaning to voyage and adventure, Carpaccio found still another occasion to proclaim the beauty of Venice. As an artist, he developed a taste for architecture and was able to suggest projects for new buildings, for example the palace with a cupola which appears in the centre of the scene of *The Ambassadors come before the King of Brittany*. In the series of St. Ursula, the balance between the perspective and the decoration of the different planes is both subtle and harmonious. In the foregrounds, the artist often used

Above and right

VITTORE CARPACCIO
The Legend of St. Ursula. The Arrival at Cologne
details
canvas, 9 x 8 ft. (280 x 255 cm)
Venice, Accademia

Following pages

The Legend of St. Ursula. Martyrdom of the Christians under Cologne and the Burial of St. Ursula
canvas, 9 x 18 ft. (271 x 561 cm)
Venice, Accademia

illusionistic feats with trompe-l'œil; at the same time he obtained impressions of distance by softening the atmosphere in the backgrounds. He knew how to depict minute everyday reality, but never allowed details to spoil his master plan. This 'architect of painting' displayed great artistry in assembling parts to form a complete, integrated picture. His mastery of mise-en-scène, the perfection with which he arranged the scenery, the actors, and the properties shown in his pictures constituted a landmark on the path that eventually led to the dynamic energy that his illustrious successors–Titian, Tintoretto, and Veronese–would build up in their paintings.

RECONCILING THE SACRED WITH THE PROFANE

The sacred approach to life so characteristic of the Middle Ages still impregnated the age of the Renaissance. However, the intellectual framework of the time was deeply concerned with man; it attempted to reconcile religious faith with secular curiosity.

In the paintings described earlier, reality is reflected by symbols, worldly pleasures do not contradict spiritual joys, science does not contradict religion, and people do not enter into conflict with each other but find ground for better understanding. The refined sensitivity that permeates these paintings is typical of Humanism.

The devout meditation depicted by Carpaccio (*The Vision of St. Augustine, c.* 1502, Scuole S. Giorgio degli Schiavoni) and the ceremonial pageant described by a follower of Gentile Bellini (*Audience of an Ambassador in an Eastern City,* Louvre) are two sides of the same subjective attitude towards art.

Carpaccio transposed the fifth-century retreat of a Latin Father of the Church into the comfortable Renaissance *studiolo* of a Venetian scholar. The Saint, clothed in a red garment and white surplice with a small cape over his shoulders, is seated at an elegant table. The seashell on the left illustrates the taste for curious objects and strange organic forms which was typical of the period. Manuscripts bound in red leather lie about and the open music scores have been identified as a sacred hymn and a popular song. Carpaccio did not omit the astrolabe sphere–the symbol of scientific research. St. Augustine is bathed in the same soft light that illuminates a bronze statue of a resurrected Christ in the central niche and the small statuette of a nude female on the shelf to the left.

In his painting, the follower of Gentile Bellini was aroused by a special preoccupation–to bring together two different worlds. He perfectly illustrated the Venetian approach to diplomacy in which delegates of two nations should prefer negotiation to confrontation. The unusual presence of a stag and a doe in the foreground may symbolise peace.

Carpaccio was one of the first to take advantage of canvas; he perfectly attuned this new support to his needs. He prepared a very

thin ground that barely covered the rough textile and lightly applied oil paint as in a sketch. He probably sought to construct a three-dimensional, clear space on which the figures would be placed afterwards, for example, in *The Vision of St. Augustine* and in his most famous canvas, *Two Courtesans* (Museo Correr). He used drawing in a purely Venetian manner to suggest pictorial effects that the completed painting would then render. This technique allowed him to create a halo around his subjects, shrouding them in a mysterious mood that did not prevent allegoric interpretations. Then the time would come for Giorgione–the creative genius!

Vittore Carpaccio
The Vision of St. Augustine
c. 1502, canvas, 57 1/4 x 72 1/4 in.
(144 x 208 cm)
Venice, Scuola S. Giorgio degli Schiavoni

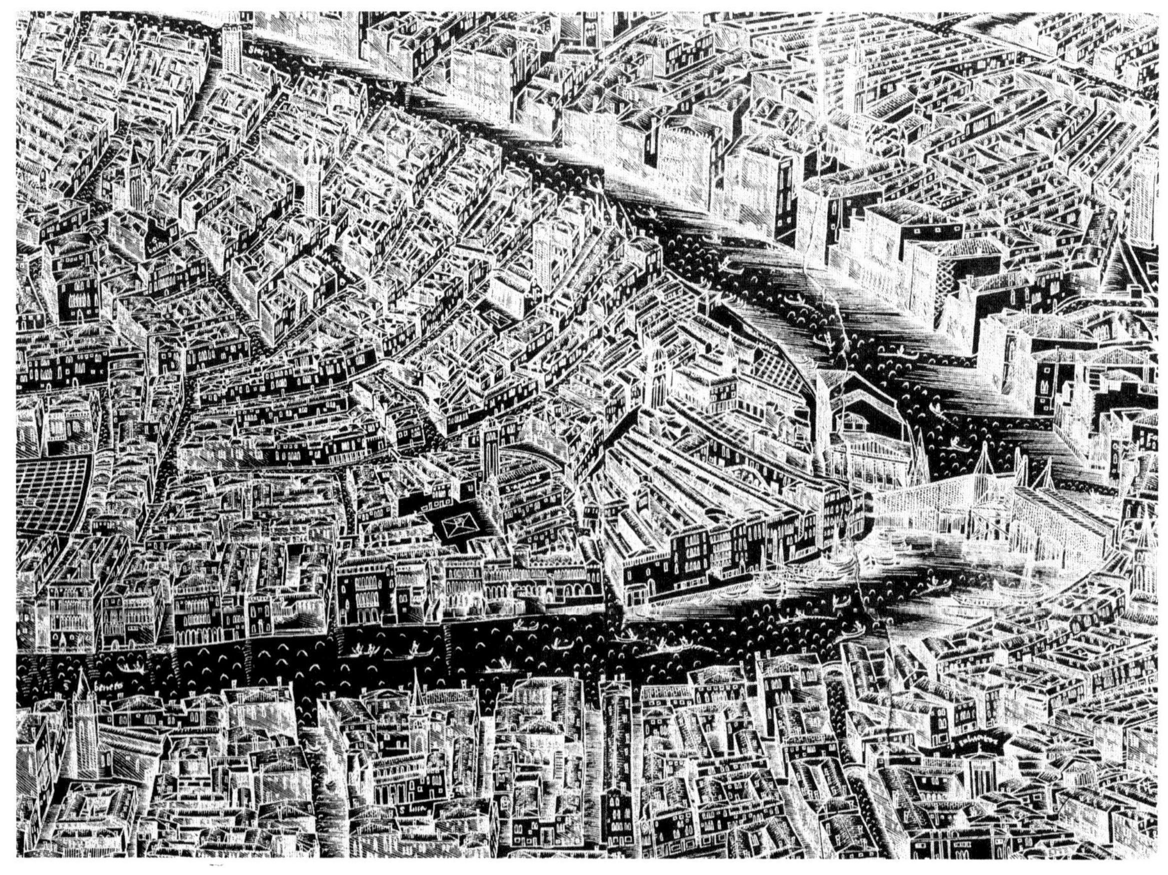

LOVE AND POETRY

GIORGIONE

Born in Castelfranco in the Veneto in 1477 or 1478, Giorgione was twenty-two or twenty-three years old when Venice, with a population of one hundred and fifty thousand, had become one of the largest cities in the world. The *Serenissima,* at the height of her glory, had accomplished her expansion and was showing off. Jacopo de' Barbari's *Bird's-eye View of Venice* in 1500 presented the city from a vantage point of pure fantasy where everything was crystalline and in good order. The Grand Canal, the *fondachi*, the palaces, the Rialto bridge had found their place for eternity, and Venice's supremacy over the sea had been secured by the galleys that cruised in front of the Giudecca.

The effects of the expanding world after the discovery of America by Christopher Columbus for the Court of Spain, and the opening up of routes to India by the Portuguese navigator Vasco da Gama had not yet challenged the splendour of the *Serenissima.* Venetian commerce with the Orient from where she brought back her riches had not been threatened. Venice did not take part in the continual feuds that embittered relations between the other Italian cities. Confirming a nearly thousand-year-old scenario, she resisted all social dissent even during adversity and escaped the confusion caused by a general weakening of authority.

Venice kept her grandeur and her inventive forces intact by introducing improvements in many fields, such as urbanisation,

Jacopo de' Barbari (c. 1450-1515
Perspective Map of Venice
1500, woodcut
Venice, Museo Correr

architecture, art collecting, and especially printing. Aldo Manuce invented the italic typeface and produced books in the octavo format–easier to carry about. Innovation remained the driving force that the Republic utilised to reinforce her prestige and cohesion.

THE FRESCOES OF FONDACO DEI TEDESCHI

The renovations of many buildings destroyed by fire became a pretext for more colourful ornamentation throughout Venice. Among these was the restoration of the facade along the Grand Canal near the Rialto bridge by the Fondaco dei Tedeschi entrusted to two young artists in 1508: Giorgione and Titian. The first was already famous at the age of thirty; the latter was his talented twenty-year-old apprentice. It was thanks to their common master Giovanni Bellini–official artist of the city–that powerful German merchants who had settled in Venice would commission the young artists to paint frescoes displaying a series of allegories on the vast panels that separate the windows of the high facade.

The salt air and the dust-laden *sirocco* wind that blows from the Sahara desert would soon destroy this wall painting. Only a few modest fragments–difficult to decipher–remain. Nonetheless, the comments that Vasari made in his *Lives of the Artists* (1550)–the first and most influential of all narrative and critical histories of art in the sixteenth century–at the time when the frescoes were still intact deserve to be repeated. At this spot, "the most beautiful and most conspicuous of the City, Giorgione went to work with no other thoughts than to prove his talent, creating figures according to his imagination. These scenes do not follow in logical sequence and do not represent the story of an illustrious person from antiquity or from modern times. I have never understood this work nor have I found anyone able to explain it to me."

That Vasari–a Florentine master both proficient in the field of art and preoccupied in sharing his erudition with the public–failed to understand the significance of Giorgione's project seems quite surprising. Vasari believed that good art should be based on good design, not on the skilful application of colour in order better to imitate nature; therefore, he regarded the Venetian approach as fundamentally misguided.

THE ENIGMA

The historical figure of Giorgione is almost a myth and our knowledge of his career is confined to a few contemporary references, yet his methods were widely adopted by most of his contemporaries. At Giorgione's death, the artists of his generation had changed their approach to designing figures and introduced a greater sense of movement in their compositions. From Vasari to the most eminent scholars of the twentieth

Alvise Vivarini (1445-1505)
St. Anthony of Padua
wood, $11^{1/2}$ x $8^{3/4}$ in. (29.5 x 22.5 cm)
Venice, Museo Correr

century, no one has resolved the Giorgione enigma. A plethora of interpretations have followed one another over the years all declaring the importance of his work in the history of art.

Although only a handful of paintings are undisputedly attributed to him, they are novel in many ways. First of all, the artist not only initiated a new technique rejecting the dry, hard, and laboured style of the Bellini School, but favoured softer outlines which gave his pictures a formidable movement more suited to depicting nature. In addition, he seems to have been the first to handle non-religious themes for private collectors. The subject matter in Giorgione's work does not convey a particularly profound meaning but shows a psychological remoteness without a learned or literary content–a tendency exhibited by almost all Venetian non-religious painting in the first half of the sixteenth century.

Giorgione broke with the traditional way of seeing, working, and selling painting in one fell swoop. Clearly, the dozen works that have been attributed to Giorgione are highly innovative. The young master began painting canvases in small dimensions and instituted working for an exclusive clientele of rich amateurs. He broke traditions when he emancipated painting from its documentary function and its historic and religious role; he breached conventions by introducing the numinous values (unconscious overtones) in a profane subject (conscious content) and deeply transformed the art of painting.

The very special ambiguity that emanates from Giorgione's works still fascinates today's amateur. Why does the observer–not contented by his first reading of the subject–feel compelled to discover some hidden significance in Giorgione's painting? Why does a closer examination of these pictures lead to more questions? Why have many interpretations of these works not dissipated the inexpressible mystery? It must be charm exerting its power!

Only five paintings can be attributed with total certainty to Giorgione. Three major works cannot be transported: *Tempesta* (Accademia), the *Three Philosophers* (*c.* 1508, Vienna) and *Sleeping Venus* (Dresden). Two others which have proved difficult to attribute–*The Pastoral Concert* (*c.* 1510, Louvre) and *The Concert* (Florence, Palazzo Pitti)–may have been painted by Giorgione or by Titian or perhaps by both of them. This has added to their fascinating beauty.

GIORGIONE (?1478-1510)
Sleeping Venus
canvas, 42 3/4 x 69 in. (108.5 x 175 cm)
Dresden, Staatliche Kunstsammlungen,
Galerie Alte Meister

For this young humanist, musician, and painter, love was without doubt the key to the hidden doors of his secret life. The premature death of this passionate poet who rejoiced in the pleasures of love *("dilettose continovamente delle cose d'amore")* was predestined. As the story goes, Giorgione died in 1510 because he refused to abandon his mistress who had become infected by the plague, and in turn caught the disease himself. The understanding of suffering, spiritual consciousness, and selfless tenderness which carried him to his death sum up the traits of his character. Such a compassionate nature confers a tragic tone *('col tempo')* and a sense of immortality to his works.

SLEEPING VENUS

The presage that death constitutes a latent threat to love pervades and illuminates Giorgione's paintings. The same kind of emotional state, expressing deep nostalgic feelings, can be felt in Rilke's Prayer:

"Oh God, give to each his own death,
Give to each the death suited to his life
Where he knew love and misery."

Botticelli was the first to liberate Venus from the grotto where she had been held prisoner for a thousand years. Crowned with hair as blond as ripened wheat, supple, pure, youthful, graceful and very Florentine, she faces man's appraisal with charming modesty. She is waiting to receive a lavish cloak that a young woman–the sister of Spring–will throw over her cold nakedness, a nudity so seductive that it inspires veneration.

Giorgione's Venus manifests the same chastity, the same aloofness, and the same seduction. Her body with its rounder, more Venetian forms, expects merely awe and adoration from love. She reclines, asleep, in a landscape worthy of her body, her hand under her head in a

Above and right

GIORGIONE
The Three Philosophers
c. 1508, canvas, 48 5/8 x 56 7/8 in.
(123.5 x 144.5 cm)
Vienna, Kunsthistorisches Museum

simple pose that painters have tried to imitate countless times but never with total success. When the beholder of the *Sleeping Venus* sees the woman and her image composed into such perfect harmony, he oscillates between the world of depiction and the world of reality. A similar harmony reigns between the goddess and the world around her and between Venus and the woman that man has the right to love. No adornment spoils the harmony of the picture. Beauty diffused in the tranquillity of sleep eludes unchaste thoughts. Venus sleeps while we fantasise.

Later on, Titian adopted the composition of Giorgione's Venus and transposed it to another decor for his *Urbino Venus* (*c.* 1538, Florence, Uffizi). Here, he robbed Venus of all her goddess-like attributes and exempted the viewer from having to use his imagination. She is awake in domestic surroundings, waiting to be dressed by a servant who is searching in a hamper for the proper attire for her mistress. Titian's domesticated Venus offers her enticements in a truly public declaration. She is a Venus at everyone's disposal. Ulrich Middledorf remarked ironically: "It's painted in a bedroom…."

Giorgione, on the contrary, guarded his secrets in silence. Silence allows the music that is awakened by emotions to be heard.

THE THREE PHILOSOPHERS

If both profane and sacred love induce inspiration, philosophy may have the same effect. The *Three Philosophers*, from the

period of the Fondaco dei Tedeschi frescoes (1508), were painted by Giorgione for his friend the painter Taddeo Contarini. The picture became the pretext for scholarly discussions on the hidden meaning–the enigmatic element of the composition. Are the three thinkers conversing with each other or each one by himself? Are they advancing three different hypotheses on the mysteries of the soul and the universe, or, do they represent the Three Kings? Even without holding the same opinions, the *Three Philosophers* seem in profound harmony with the world around them. The bright colours of the group in the foreground progressively blend into the natural landscape behind, relating man to its environment.

This promenade, however, may suggest other interpretations, some of which Giorgione evoked in the *Three Ages of Man* (Florence, Pitti). Here, wisdom is not the prerogative of age and no one is the master of harmony. The young seated philosopher on the left is contemplating the secrets of human nature, still fettered by its bonds; the mature philosopher in the centre of the group is not hampered by objects that might lead his convictions astray. The old man on the right is holding the proof of his erudition in a book whose author is not divulged and in which his knowledge may be immortalised.

Of all of Giorgione's works, the one which has received by far the most admiration and comment is the *Tempesta* (1506-1508, Accademia). Unfortunately, it is impossible to take a good photograph of it today because it was placed, after restoration, behind a thick pane of glass. We know the name of Giorgione's close friend who commissioned the painting–the young and rich merchant Gabriele Vendramin–and also the fact that it was hung in his palace during the artist's lifetime.

Nonetheless, many questions still remain with regard to this work. Does the scene depict the birth of Venus? Does it suggest unrequited love between a gypsy girl and a shepherd? Should it be interpreted (a recent x-ray revealed the presence of a naked woman seated by the water painted beneath the actual figure of the shepherd) as an allegory of the two Venuses–the divine and the earthly?

CHALLENGING THE GODS

When a painting has an inspiring and exalting effect upon us, we can assume that the artist has probed deep down into his own inspiration, far beyond the subject-matter that he has treated in his work. If the painter feels compelled to create, it is not only to compete with his rivals, but also to be regarded as a poet engaged in an intuitive quest to unveil the fundamental forces that drive the world.

With the allegory of the *Flaying of Marsyas*, Titian in his later years may have chosen to render homage to Giorgione, his master and friend. It was not Marsyas' audacity in engaging Apollo in a contest that

Left

TITIAN
The Flaying of Marsyas
c. 1570, canvas, 7 x 6 1/2 ft.
(212 x 207 cm)
Kromeriz (Czech Republic), Statnzamek

Antonio Zanchi (1631-1722)
The Plague in Venice
1666, canvas, 39 x 53 1/8 in.
(99 x 135 cm)
Vienna, Kunsthistorisches Museum

brought about the satyr's punishment, but his excessive ambition. The satyr was not being criticised for trying to obtain the unobtainable, but probably for succeeding. Such a success turned out to be unacceptable, for it would perturb the harmonious arrangement of the world. The torture, beyond the individual punishment, was inflicted upon Marsyas in order to protect the whole of humanity.

Who sets the limits to man's power?

This question was debated by the Humanists of the Renaissance. Giorgione and Titian must have been confronted with this kind of discussion in an atmosphere full of drama. On account of the plague, man's expectations were constantly thwarted by a peril so frightful that artists hesitated to represent it. It was only some time later, in the second half of the seventeenth century, that painters such as Antonio Zanchi, in 1666, undertook to depict the plague on their canvases.

It is important to notice that the new painting techniques Giorgione devised greatly contribute to the perfection of his work. While his immediate predecessors were still very much influenced by tempera–a medium that necessitated careful planning and required pigments to be applied in thin layers–Giorgione devised a freer oil technique characterised by the use of thicker layers of paint, allowing colours to interpenetrate and blend with each other and achieve subtle effects of transparency. Thus, he experimented with a practice that his successors would perfect all through the sixteenth century.

Moreover, Giorgione was the first–Vasari criticised him for it–to refrain from using drawings on paper to prepare his compositions although his method of application allowed him to modify his first projects at will. Painting directly on the canvas without any prior constraints became a creative discovery more than just an accomplishment.

GIORGIONE
La Vecchia (Old Woman)
1502-1503, canvas, 68 3/4 x 23 1/4 in.
(68 x 59 cm)
Venice, Accademia

Left

GIORGIONE
Young Man with an Arrow
c. 1505, wood, 19 x 16 1/2 in.
(48 x 42 cm)
Vienna, Kunsthistorisches Museum

FROM LAURA TO THE VECCHIA

Should Giorgione's life and achievements be read in another light? When *Laura* (c. 1506, Vienna) and *La Vecchia* (1502-1503, Accademia) are juxtaposed, they show how Giorgione condensed the entire destiny of woman into two portraits. The apprehensive look on the face of the still-innocent young woman forms a contrast with the resigned mien of the old woman of experience who knows that the passage of time cannot be stopped, but that she has to come to terms with it: *'col tempo'* ('with time').

The evocative power of Giorgione's work influenced all the arts reaching beyond the field of painting, inspiring even poets. The American novelist Mark Helprin in *A Soldier of the Great War* (1993) wrote: "As the world darkened before him and the wind rose, Giorgione felt his own death and the death of everyone and everything he loved. He understood dissolution. He saw ruin and night. He saw the future of prosperous and proud cities, of the arches, bridges and upright walls."

Unquestionably, the conflicting circumstances that took place during Giorgione's life such as the carefree celebration of religious and popular holidays and the terrible insecurity from the threat of the plague should be taken into consideration. Facing these acute contradictions which characterised the first years of the sixteenth century in Venice, how could he have envisioned a future that was not fundamentally dramatic? There was nothing between laughter and tears; relief would only come later. The *Serenissima*, spared for several dozen years from the plague and at the height of her commercial ascendancy, would live her greatest period of splendour in a state of grace. But Giorgione was no longer on the shores of the lagoon. He left to posterity the mysterious image of a *Young Man with an Arrow* (1505, Vienna)–an image of immortality.

Right

GIORGIONE
Laura
canvas,
$17^{1}/_{8}$ x $13^{1}/_{4}$ in.
(41 x 33.6 cm)
Vienna,
Kunsthistorisches
Museum

Below

GIORGIONE
The Old Woman
detail
see p. 111

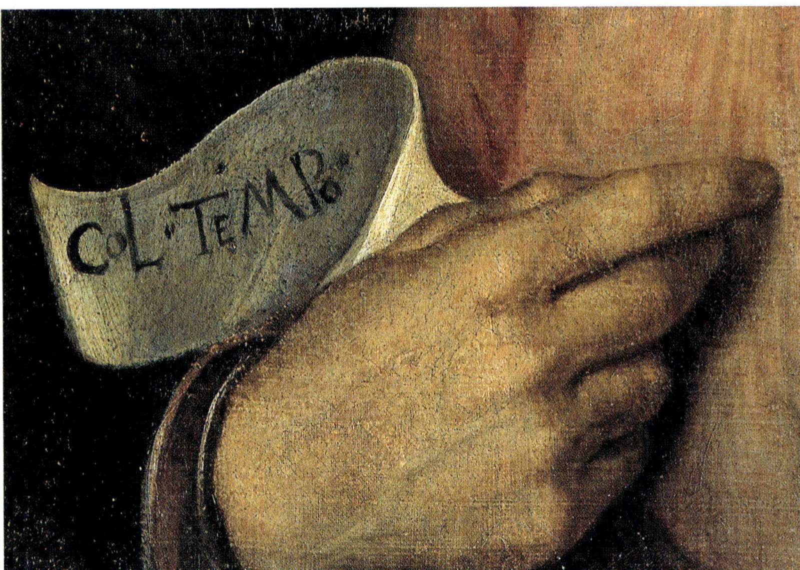

A CHILD OF VENICE

TINTORETTO

Referred to as Titian's century for a long time, the sixteenth century also produced, according to Vasari, "the most awesome mind that painting ever knew: Tintoretto." Jacopo Robusti was born in Venice in 1518. His father, originally from Tuscany, worked as a silk dyer in a modest neighbourhood of the city. It was because of this trade that Jacopo got the name of Il Tintoretto, son of a dyer. He painted both religious and lay works commissioned by private patrons and the State. According to some sources he was a pupil of Titian for a short time. In Elie Faure's opinion: "Some analogies can be drawn between Tintoretto and Titian, who at first glance resemble each other just as Veronese resembles them, and as, for a matter of fact, all the Venetians resemble one another. In comparing, for example, the juxtaposition of forms–both luminous and sombre–under the red sunlight on the horizon of the sea, even if their language expresses the same images and the same resonance, there exists, nonetheless, almost an antagonism of soul among these artists."[1]

It is easier to grasp Tintoretto by studying his work than trying to understand him through the story of his life–as is the case with many of the other painters of this era. The mystery surrounding this artist has given free rein to speculation. In one of the most pointed articles

TINTORETTO
Susanna and the Elders
detail
see p. 128

1. E. Faure, *Histoire de l'art. L'art renaissant*, 1986.

Tintoretto (Jacopo Robusti, 1518-1594)
St Nicholas of Bari
c. 1592, canvas, 45 x 22 in.
(114 x 56 cm)
Vienna, Kunsthistorisches Museum

that he wrote on sixteenth-century Venetian artists, Sartre (*Les Temps Modernes*, November 1957) offered an interpretation of one particular event: "...everything began badly around 1530 when the young man entered Titian's studio as an apprentice. It only took a few days for the celebrated older master to discover Tintoretto's genius and Titian threw him right out the door."

This anecdote has been reported so many times and with such insistence that it has become a legend. No material has come forth to confirm the episode nor has anything ever contradicted it.

From the age of twelve when this misfortune took place until the age of twenty no one knew what had become of the budding artist. It has been suggested that he was self taught. This is a farfetched assumption for he could not have learned the rules, the devices, or the techniques of his trade without working under the wing of a mature master. "A painter about whom we know nothing, except that he was not Titian" wrote Sartre.

Nonetheless, Jacopo Robusti, who rapidly made a name for himself, developed an impressive style. In his first large canvas he already displayed the fundamental components of his art, upsetting the classic layout of form and light. He was resolved to illustrate the narrative in a different way in order to make the spectator feel the thrill and tense drama of the events he painted. His compositions demonstrate a remarkable sensibility for spatial and dynamic values and an exceptional skill in the use of colour and three-dimensional forms. Both his religious and profane works convey a sense of everyday life to the scenes, making them immediately accessible on an emotional level.

We know some precise details about Tintoretto's working habits, so novel were they that they brought criticism from his contemporaries. This uninhibited approach to painting may account for the inventiveness of his compositions. In a small room transformed into a studio, he reproduced wax models, as well as studies from life and from casts of classical sculpture and statues of Michelangelo. He built small decor in perspective like a real theatre stage, placing miniature figurines dressed in pieces of fabric so that the folds of clothing would capture the light; then he set candles around the figurines in order to obtain visual movement. Finally, he transposed these scenes on to canvas.

Tintoretto wrote a prescription for his own use on the wall of his studio: "The drawing of Michelangelo and the colouring of Titian." He was not however a great colourist, although he often used enticing, even strange, colours. But his approach to colour displayed the general tendency of this period with a clear disengagement from any direct relation to visual experience. Only very rarely in Tintoretto's work do we see the reality of space and air characteristic of Titian's late work.

Tintoretto's compositions were built around one desire: to treat narrative subjects. At thirty, he painted *The Miracle of the Slave* for

Above and right

Tintoretto
Danae
details
c. 1580, canvas, 56 x 64 in.
(142 x 182.5 cm)
Lyon, musée des Beaux-Arts

Danae, the mother of Perseus, was visited by Zeus in the form of a shower of gold. A humble maidservant tries to catch some of the gold in her pinafore.

the Scuola di S. Marco. This work surprises and even disconcerts with the extreme dramatic effect that involves the viewer in the action taking place on the canvas. Seized by an insatiable compulsion to create and animated by a need to compensate for his lower-class upbringing, he concentrated on achieving a pictorial ideal in a continual unsatisfied search. Tintoretto sought to evoke what was 'imaginable' more than what was 'natural'. He organised within the confines of his canvas a mise-en-scène with a clever use of lighting, often from two different sources–one natural, the other artificial. This was only one of his devices.

Another ruse was his system of handling clients and competitors. Through attentive observation and experience, Tintoretto learned to imitate the styles of Veronese or Pordenone and to keep abreast of the most popular themes. He would execute them and at a lower price! He felt that Venice, never having offered him an official position like the one held by Titian (and that would later be transmitted to Veronese), owed him more than she was giving to the other artists at the time. He was the only real Venetian and he harboured this naive sentiment to justify his demands. He was the only true native of Venice, not Giorgione, who had come from Castelfranco, or Titian from the Dolomites, or Veronese from Verona. Born in and never having left the *Serenissima*, and from a modest family–thus more deserving–Tintoretto sought an esteem that he could measure with the number of commissions that he could drum up. To achieve his ends, he chose the path that seemed to him the most favourable and sought work at the *scuole*–the confraternities in charge of distributing money to the poor and devoted to the embellishment of their own buildings.

TINTORETTO ENTERS THE SCUOLE

Tintoretto thus became a protégé of the dignitaries in charge of various *scuole*. In 1550, he married Faustina, the daughter of Marco Episcopi, head of the Scuola di S. Marco. On May 31, 1564, Giovanni Battista Tornielli, in charge of the Scuola di S. Rocco, commissioned Tintoretto to decorate the oval centre of the ceiling of the Albergo Room (formerly the dining hall). On June 22, Tintoretto gave the painting–a representation of the Glory of St. Roch–to the Scuola.

How did the artist accomplish such a feat in only three weeks? Tintoretto must have benefited from a privileged situation with the *scuole* and there was certainly nothing controversial about his talent; but his forwardness and rampant appetite for notoriety were not in good taste and he was unable to bridle his ambition. He sought and often obtained work without scruples, amid the envy, anger, and calumny of his rivals. As soon as he obtained the exact measurements of a work to be executed, he would rush to outdo his competitors who were all busy working on their preliminary sketches. Tintoretto would surreptitiously execute an almost finished work and keep it hidden behind a piece of cardboard until the moment that it was to be shown to the judges. On the fixed day, each artist would present the sketch of his project. When Tintoretto's turn came, he would remove the cardboard and uncover his near-completed piece. It is easy to imagine the commotion that this caused. Tintoretto would explain that a sketch might be subject to an inaccurate interpretation and that, while he was on the job, he preferred to see it through. To take the matter even further, he would flaunt his head-start over the other competitors and even more so, over his patrons: "But if my work does not suit you, I will offer it; not to you, Sirs, but to St. Roch, your patron." He knew that it was written into the statutes of the confraternity that a pious donation could not be refused. The affair was therefore concluded and the painting registered among the belongings of the Scuola. "On this day, the undersigned Jacopo Tintoretto, painter, has made us the gift of a painting; he has not requested any payment and has promised to complete the work if it is deemed necessary and claims to be satisfied." And the artist wrote in turn: *"Io Jachomo Tentoretto pitor contento...."*

In these troubled times with pressure from the Turkish and Italian armies and new outbreaks of the plague, the religious holidays and the Carnival–that went on for six months of the year–were not enough to assuage fear.

As if stimulated by the prestige that other artists enjoyed, Tintoretto devoted himself entirely to his work. Nothing could slow him down nor relieve his thirst to create. After the success of the decoration of S. Rocco's ceiling, he undertook a commission to cover the walls and other ceilings of the Scuola. For twenty-three years, from 1564 to 1587, working alone, often encouraged by musicians who accompanied him, he gave himself over entirely to his trade.

In the sixteenth century, great artists such as Tintoretto and Veronese held their own, gallantly. Thus, Titian had to share his century with them, yet his rank was never challenged.

A CINEMATOGRAPHIC VISION OF THE CRUCIFIXION

The *Crucifixion* (1565), one of Tintoretto's major works for the Scuola, is considered by many as his greatest masterpiece. He may have felt the need to apologise for his offensive behaviour during the attribution of the oval ceiling and he felt that he should demonstrate with this new commission an ability to carry out a job without cynicism.

When John Ruskin described and commented on the extraordinary architecture, sculpture and painting of Venice for nineteenth-century English tourists, he dwelled on the Scuola di S. Rocco: "As regards the pictures which it contains, it is one of the three most precious buildings in Italy; buildings, I mean, consistently decorated with a series of paintings

TINTORETTO
The Crucifixion
1565, canvas, 17$^{1/2}$ x 40 ft.
(536 x 1224 cm)
Venice, Scuola di S. Rocco
see details pp. 122-123

at the time of their erection, and still exhibiting that series in its original order. I suppose there can be little question but that the three most important edifices of this kind in Italy are the Sistine Chapel, the Campo Santo of Pisa, and the Scuola di S. Rocco at Venice."

Ruskin analysed in detail each one of the sixty-two paintings that were hung in the building. He was literally reduced to silence in front of the *Crucifixion*: "I must leave this picture to work its will on the spectator; for it is beyond all analysis, and above all praise."

The enormous canvas of the *Crucifixion,* signed by Tintoretto in the bottom left-hand corner, occupies the entire width of the far wall of the Albergo Room at the Scuola. The painting, more than an evocation of the death of Christ, is truly a spectacle. The focal point of the mise-en-scène is the crucified Christ silhouetted against a cloudy sky with the group of afflicted at the foot of the Cross among a tumultuous crowd. The onlookers are assembled into several groups according to precise construction lines; the foot of the Cross is the pivot of a fan-like composition suggested by the ladders and the crosses that have not yet been erected for the two thieves. The lighting effect gives the work a powerful dynamic. Groups of horsemen on each side of the scene are more strongly lit than the prostrate figures in the centre, drawing the eye towards the exterior of the ellipse formed by the different figures. Noticeably, many of them are only there by chance, taken by surprise in their daily occupations. Moreover, the repetition of pinks, greys and blues, with a silvery moiré running through the whole composition are in contrast with the dark clothing of the woman in supplication beneath Christ on the Cross.

The shocking effect of the opposition of light and shade, of nearness and distance, and by the lack of harmony in gestures and movements was intended to draw the observer–as fascinated by the work as by the event–into the scene where he would participate in the drama. There is nothing overdone in this prodigious construction. Tintoretto composed a superb symphonic movement of coloured volumes which painted a story readily understood even by the illiterate. Elie Faure commented on this particular treatment:

"This permanent spatial drama, makes me think of cinematography, more than what it is now, but what it should strive for. The action in the background never ceases to participate actively with the general movement; in return, the general movement participates with the tragedy taking place.... Three hundred years before it was invented, Tintoretto–although his medium was a static one–anticipated the motion picture in the visual symphony that we expect from him...."[1]

1. E. Faure, *op. cit.*

Tintoretto
The Nativity
c. 1576, canvas, 18 x 15 ft.
(542 x 455 cm)
Venice, Scuola di S. Rocco

Curious example of a Nativity displayed on two different levels: an earthly one for the shepherds and a divine one for the Holy Family.

TINTORETTO
The Fall of Manna
c. 1592, canvas, 12 x 19 ft.
(377 x 576 cm)
Venice, Church of S. Giorgio Maggiore

SUSANNA: THE REVERSAL OF A SITUATION

As we have already pointed out with regard to *The Miracle of the Slave*, Tintoretto decided to abandon the beaten tracks of his predecessors. With all his talent as innovator, he had chosen to explore the feelings of tension and excitement within dramatic happenings while under the sway of his own anxiety and sensuality. He refused to be concerned with technical perfection but devoted himself to showing things in a new light, striving to explore new ways of representing the legends and myths of the past. This romantic creator far ahead of his time and infatuated with his trade was gifted with the ability to improvise. Captivated by music, he liked to have musicians accompany him while he executed his acrobatic brushstrokes, all the while fighting in an unequal combat against the decline that slowly eroded the *Serenissima*. He pitted his know-how against the uncertainty of his future.

It was in such an atmosphere that Tintoretto must have painted *Susanna and the Elders* (Vienna) in 1555. We cannot miss noticing how this work differs from the many others that represented this Biblical allegory throughout the sixteenth century. While other artists depicted a shrinking, fearful Susanna when confronted by the elders, Tintoretto painted her pleasantly contemplating her reflection in a mirror, self-possessed and entirely preoccupied with her own beauty. She has somehow transferred to the old men all the sins for which she may be guilty!

This reversal of situation is underlined by Tintoretto's dynamic spatial invention. On the right, we see the beauty of a nude female in all her splendour bathed in a strong light, as well as the limpid pool of water; her flesh and the objects which surround her are treated with the same sensuality. A linear perspective draws the eye into the mysterious depths of the garden that is separated from the shadows of some wild woods by a high trellised wall decorated with caryatids. On the left, a screen dotted with flowers delimits the cramped space where the old men are ready to spring out of hiding and demand that she give herself to them. With his handling of composition alone, the painter has voluntarily suspended the outcome of the drama for an instant. The composure of Susanna in total solitude and the tumultuous throng ascending Golgotha *(The Crucifixion)* are the two faces of Tintoretto's art.

"Tintoretto is the most truth-revealing of all the Venetians. His lyricism belongs to the soil. Venice, the resplendent, lives in him surely, the theatrical and romantic Venice...."[1]

TINTORETTO
Susanna and the Elders
1560, canvas, $57^{3}/4$ x $76^{1}/4$ in.
(146.6 x 193.6 cm)
Vienna, Kunsthistorisches Museum
details pp. 114, 130-131

1. E. Faure, *op. cit.*

THE MARRIAGE AT CANA, A POPULAR VERSION

In 1561, before taking on the wild project for the decoration of the Scuola di S. Rocco, Tintoretto had shown the originality of his art of composition in a version of *The Marriage at Cana* for the Church of S. Maria della Salute. A following chapter will bring us to Veronese's rendition of the same theme painted two years later for the Benedictine dining hall at S. Giorgio Maggiore.

In Tintoretto's popular version of the first miracle performed by Christ, the spiritual context of the event does not seem particularly daunting to the guests, all the more so since Christ's presence is discrete and He is seated at the far end of the table. To give life to his work, the artist multiplied the sources of light; a diffused lighting from the sky pours in through the high windows in the left-hand background and a direct light seems to surge from an invisible projector illuminating the figures in the foreground who are enjoying a simple gathering of friends. The miracle has been rendered matter-of-fact and the symbolism has been integrated into reality giving a strong sense of verisimilitude to the scene.

Tintoretto
The Marriage at Cana
1561, canvas, 14 x 18 ft. (435 x 545 cm)
Venice, Church of S. Maria della Salute
details pp. 132-133

FROM THE REDENROTE TO THE SALUTE

PALLADIO AND LONGHENA

In the fifteenth century at the time when explorers, navigators, and conquistadors were discovering new territories, Venice was no longer satisfied with her small parcel of land on the lagoon. She began to look toward the *terra firma* which she had turned her back on since her origins, preferring to gain her wealth from the sea and the Orient. It was as if she were suddenly aware of having fulfilled her obligations and that she had secured her illustrious standing for eternity. She could now absorb neighbouring regions.

Tintoretto's desire to render culture more accessible to the masses and his urge to decorate the walls and ceilings of Venetian buildings contrasted with the aspirations of the patriciate to move toward territorial expansion. However, the rich Venetians did not shift their interests outside the city before putting the last touch to the splendid decor that they would hand down to posterity.

As mentioned in an earlier chapter, Sansovino, when exiled to Venice after the Sack of Rome, was given carte blanche to decorate and redesign the city. We have already discussed his work on the Piazzetta S. Marco. His other architectural achievements include the Church of S. Francisco della Vigna, the Zecca (Mint), the Palazzo Dolfin, as well as the alignment of the handsome, low-budget industrial buildings *(fabbriche nuove)* along the Rialto. Considered as a turning point between the Early and High Renaissance styles of architecture, Sansovino's creations forged the

Left and following page

Andrea Palladio (1508-1580)
The Cloister of S. Giorgio Maggiore
Venice

way for new projects and other superb innovations, taken on successively by Andrea Palladio in the sixteenth century and Baldassare Longhena a century later.

THE ARCHITECT OF VENICE'S TERRA FIRMA

For three hundred years, Venice found rich agricultural land in the colonised islands–Corfu, Crete, and Euboea–along the maritime routes to Constantinople, Syria, and Egypt. When Venice lost most of her colonies, she sought farmland that she could cultivate closer to home and exploited the Veneto. The Venetians accomplished this while respecting the principles that had established their domination over the Mediterranean world, such as profitability based on methods of sound management and ostentation, for they felt that only the greatest display of beauty could help them maintain their power.

Although there is no room in history for coincidence, several major events took place in 1508, the year Palladio was born in Padua. First of all Venice lost mastery over the seas to the Portuguese and then suffered set-backs on the mainland under pressure from the European armies.

Andrea di Pietro della Gondola, the son of a local miller, had a profound influence on architecture. His prestige that spread over all of Europe, well beyond Venice and the Veneto, was considerable. He accomplished an intimate union between Roman classical and High Renaissance architecture and inaugurated the Baroque era. He was the first and the only genius–as Goethe would remark–who knew how to reinterpret forms from antiquity into contemporary formulae. Palladio turned to antiquity less as a model than as the key to a harmonic language to create a perfect balance between culture and taste. In other words, he nourished his inspiration with what he had learned from ancient architecture. Palladio succeeded in achieving a greater unity between the internal harmony of a building and the setting in which it was included.

At the age of thirteen, he entered an apprenticeship with the stonemason Cavazza da Sossano in Padua. In 1524, he joined the guild of masons and stonecutters of Vicenza and was hired by the famous studio of Giovanni di Giacomo da Porlezza at Pedemuro. He worked there for more than ten years, completing his knowledge of different materials and developing his sense of perfection for detail. In 1538, he met the highly esteemed Count Trissino, a humanist and poet, who introduced him to the notability of Vicenza and would become his protector, mentor, and patron.

Between 1541 and 1546, several trips to Rome offered Palladio the occasion to master his trade and permit him to deepen his knowledge of Roman and contemporary architecture. It was not until 1545 that Trissino began to call him 'Palladio' after Pallas Athena, patron of the arts. Palladio lived up to his new name.

In the fifties, Palladio executed his first commissions for the rich Vincentine bourgeois, as well as for Venetian patricians. In 1555, he went to Venice to build a cloister for the convent of S. Maria della Carità. Here, the architect reproduced an antique Roman house on a monumental scale. Vasari noted in 1568 that the building was designed "in imitation of the houses which the ancients used to build." Only two bays remain today and this fragment of the cloister has been integrated into the Accademia delle Belle Arti and bears testimony to the 'classical' phase of Palladio's interventions.

In 1558, the reconstruction of the Church of S. Pietro di Castello was entrusted to him. He created the plans for the project that would be faithfully executed by his pupils, Smeraldi and Grapiglia. In 1559, shortly thereafter on the banks of the Brenta, he built one of his most beautiful villas–the Villa Foscari–better known as the Malcontenta, the name of the small town where it is found outside Venice. It is a villa whose architecture was directly inspired by Greek temples. In order to place the principal facade towards the river, Palladio broke with tradition and faced the villa to the North. The *salone* was lit from a large thermal window forming a wall of light. In his handling of the interior of the villa, he systematically juxtaposed spaces that fit into each other without transition, achieving harmony and perfect balance between the different parts. Palladio, who devised a style borrowed from the architecture of the antique temple with columned porticoes surmounted by pediments, produced a monumental architecture that blended gracefully into the surroundings and reflected the stately sobriety appreciated by his noble patrons.

PALLADIO
Facade of the Church of S. Giorgio Maggiore
Venice

Left

PALLADIO
Villa La Malcontenta on the Brenta

The frescoes by Zelotti and Franco were executed from the architect's drawings.

SAN GIORGIO MAGGIORE AND IL REDENTORE: A NEW IMAGE OF VENICE

Then, ground was broken for the architectural complex of S. Giorgio Maggiore. The church and the monastery were set on an island across from the Doge's Palace and formed a startling contrast with the edifices on the other side of the Canale di S. Marco. The Church of S. Giorgio Maggiore was place in such a way as to be admired from the Canal where it reflects harmony between the white ashlars, the red brick and the roofs. In the eighteenth century a campanile was added in reference to the one in the Piazza S. Marco.

Here, Palladio superimposed two classic temple fronts, one based on the height of the nave and the other on that of the aisles in a prefiguration of the interior which was laid out with a Latin-cross plan in an imitation of an early Christian basilica. The facade of the church is in perfect harmony with the interior, intended as a re-creation of the hall of a Roman bath. The light falling from large mullioned, semi-circular openings–in imitation of *thermae* windows–illuminates the immaculate

BALDASSARE LONGHENA (1598-1682)
The Library of S. Giorgio Maggiore
1641-1653
Venice, S. Giorgio Maggiore

The shelving was carved by the German sculptor Franz Pauch (c. 1665-1671).

Right

PALLADIO
The Church of S. Giorgio Maggiore
interior views
Venice

whitewashed walls and pilasters contrasting with the grey of the Istrian stone used for the columns, the architectural accents, and the entablature. The result is breathtaking in its lightness, airiness, and spaciousness.

Towards the end of his life, Palladio was given the occasion to expound his philosophy of architecture. On September 4, 1576, in the hopes of saving Venice from the plague that was once again exterminating a considerable part of the population, the Senate decided to build a votive church to Christ the Redeemer. The terrible epidemic of 1575-1576 killed 50,000 of the 175,000 inhabitants. Titian's mistress died, then his daughter, and finally the artist himself. Incense was burned in the streets. People went out wearing masks shaped like a bird's head with a long beak filled with aromatic substances. Coins were dipped in vinegar and houses were disinfected. Nothing did any good. During these terrible years, Venice suffered atrociously and, as if this were not enough, two fires burned down the Doge's Palace, in 1571 and then in 1577. Works by the Bellini, Carpaccio, Veronese, and Titian were destroyed. The battle of Lepanto that Venice (allied with the Pope and with Spain) won against the Turks–thanks to the cunning of Admiral Sebastiano Venier–was not sufficient to restore faith and courage to the Venetians.

THE BATTLE OF LEPANTO: A VICTORY EN TROMPE-L'ŒIL

The naval battle that the Christians of the Holy League fought against the Turks was one of the greatest ever held in the Mediterranean Sea. The allies deployed two hundred and fourteen war ships with superior firing power–more than half of these had been built at the Arsenal in Venice–against two hundred and thirty Turkish galleys. On

TINTORETTO
Doge Sebastiano Venier
detail
c. 1575, canvas, 55 3/8 x 32 7/8 in.
(140.5 x 83.5 cm)
Vienna, Kunsthistorisches Museum

The Doge led the Venetian fleet at the Battle of Lepanto (1571), pictured in the background.

Right

The Great Council of Venice
late sixteenth-century manuscript
Paris, Bibliothèque nationale

Celebration of the Lepanto victory over the Turks, presided over by Sebastiano Venier.

October 7, 1571, outside the port of Lepanto to the Southwest of the Greek coast, the Turkish troops met with defeat. Although Venice had won the battle and deserved credit for the great victory that was received with a general outburst of joy throughout Christendom, she had lost the war. Dalmatia and the Ionian Islands of Zante and Corfu had been saved, but Cyprus fell into enemy hands. Then, Venice became unsure of her command over the seas and began to lose her aplomb.

Efforts were made, however, to delay the fatal hour. Artists such as Tintoretto and Veronese, by glorifying the fleet's exploits, encouraged the Venetians to regain the confidence in themselves that had always been their most stalwart trait. Unfortunately, these endeavours would not be enough to turn the tide of history, and Venice received a direct blow to her spirit. The victory of Lepanto was a false victory. In the face of decline, the Venetians turned to piety.

If the plague were the divine punishment inflicted on an amoral city over-preoccupied with its own image, was it not time to appease divine wrath? Was it not urgent to adopt a more humble attitude and glorify devotion? With this in mind, city councillors devoted themselves once more to religious architecture.

On May 3, 1577 the construction of the Church of Il Redentore on the Island of the Giudecca began. Palladio completed this project, working as both city planner and architect. With this great achievement, he created the most picturesque landscape of Venice. He designed the temple-like church with three different functions in mind: as the fulfilment of a vow, as a presbytery for the monks, and as a vessel to which processions could wend their way. The final highlight was the Convent of the Zittelle (spinsters), a home for poor Venetian girls, which Palladio designed in 1580, several months before his death. His plans for these buildings as well as for the Church of Il Redentore were respected to some extent by those who carried them out under the authority of Antonio Da Ponte, the architect who had rebuilt the Rialto Bridge between 1588 and 1591.

In 1557, a lengthy competition took place between the greatest architects of the century–Michelangelo, Sansovino and Palladio–over the stone reconstruction of the Rialto Bridge. A lack of funds, as well as the spirited arguments aroused by the various projects, delayed the construction for thirty years. The question disputed was whether it should be a bridge with three arches or five arches or, in spite of the risk, a bridge with just a single arch. We know that the last option was finally adopted and that the architect appointed to carry it out was Da Ponte.

M.D.LXXI.VI.KAL.MART.
ANNO.MAGNÆ.NAVALIS.
VICTORIÆ.DEI.GRA.
CONTRA.TVRCAS.

Johann Zeckel
Commemorative Monstrance for Lepanto
1708
Ingolstadt, Maria de Victoria Kirche

On the left page, Pope Pius V medallion.

THE SALUTE: A BAROQUE TOUCH

Still missing on the Grand Canal, however, was an essential masterpiece which would be added fifty years later. Venice would not be herself without the baroque touch of the Basilica della Salute, the major achievement of Baldassare Longhena. The architect, born in 1598 at the end of the prolific sixteenth century, came from a family of sculptors.

Finished in 1654, the Basilica followed in Palladio's footsteps, completing an ideal circle of churches: St. Mark's, St. George's, and the Redeemer. There, Longhena achieved an original cohesion: severity inside the edifice and exuberance on the outside. Indeed, the whole project was revolutionary. In designing the church, Longhena followed a centralised octagonal plan. He raised the building on a platform with a flight of steps at the front and crowned it with an giant cupola supported by immense ear-like scrolls *(orecchioni)* which served as buttresses. Outside, he clothed the walls with six architectural facades, each adorned with pillars, pediments, niches, and statues. Influenced by Palladio's Teatro Olimpico, he conceived

TITIAN
St. Mark with Saints Sebastian, Roch, Cosmas, and Damian
c. 1511, wood, 89 x 45 1/2 in.
(226 x 146 cm)
Venice, S. Maria della Salute

Left

BALDASSARE LONGHENA
The Church of S. Maria della Salute
Venice

the magnificent entrance way as a *scenae frons*, topping the pediment and the spaces between the columns with statues.

At the time he was working on the Salute, Longhena was commissioned by the great Venetian families to renovate their palaces. In 1647, he earned an even greater name, with his design for the Palazzo Belloni-Battagia, one of the most beautiful buildings of the seventeenth century with its well-balanced facade. He then continued with a magnificent palazzo on the Grand Canal. The Ca' Pesaro is unparalleled in Venetian Baroque architecture with its monumental structure accentuated by heavy rustication, rich sculptural features, and ample use of columns.

Above, left, and preceding pages

Baldassare Longhena
The Church of S. Maria della Salute
Venice

Above, left, and preceding pages

Palladio
The Church of Redentore
Venice, La Giudecca

Doorway and interior views of this church consecrated to the Redeemer.

THE MARRIAGE AT CANA

Andrea Palladio began to work on the Island of S. Giorgio, planning out the church like the interior of a villa in such a way that the light would underline the tension between the ribs, the cornices, the capitals and the windows. The commission to build this edifice, however, was not given to Palladio until later. In the meantime he had been asked to undertake the renovation of the monks' refectory. Palladio, therefore, called on his friend Paolo Caliari who was born in 1528 in Verona–hence his nickname of Veronese–as he had a few years earlier while he was building villas in the country for Venetian nobles and dignitaries. The painter's command of illusion reached its height in the decoration of Palladio's Villa Barbaro at Maser where the allegorical anecdotes were cleverly permeated with scenes of everyday life. Veronese can also be looked upon as a painter of landscapes, drawing profound inspiration from nature as demonstrated by the vigorous country scenes with which he enlivened the rather sedate monochrome panels of architectural decorations in some of the rooms of the Villa Barbaro.

The two artists shared the same limitless attachment to a type of architectural beauty. They both agreed on Palladio's definition: "Beauty will result from form, from the relationship of each part to the whole, of the parts among themselves, and all of these together, so that the edifice becomes a complete, well-finished body whose every limb is necessary to reach the final objective."[1]

VERONESE
The Marriage at Cana
details
see p. 168

1. Andrea Palladio *I Quattro Libri dell'Architettura,* Venice 1570.

ANTONELLO DA MESSINA
Portrait of a Condottiere
1475, canvas, $14^{1/4}$ x $14^{7/8}$ in.
(36.2 x 30 cm)
Paris, musée du Louvre

Right

ANDREA DEL VERROCCHIO (1435-1488)
Monument to the Condottiere Bartolomeo Colleoni (1400-1476)
Bronze
Venice, Campo SS. Giovanni e Paolo

Verrocchio's masterpiece is the most famous equestrian statue of the Renaissance. The statue was completed and erected in 1479.

Not only did the painter add an element of intense jubilation to the elegant structures built by the architect, he integrated the simplified and harmonious forms of Palladian architecture in most of his larger compositions, whether religious or secular in theme.

With the works that he painted on the wall of the monks' refectory, Veronese did not hesitate to employ all the fanciful inventiveness of trompe-l'œil, increasing the true abstraction of form that dominated his work. The highly visual quality of Veronese's art, with its tendency towards decoration rather than emotional expressiveness, set him apart from Tintoretto, although Veronese's example profoundly marked the course of painting in Venice, especially during the eighteenth century. Although receptive to the most audacious spatial experiments conducted by artists like Pordenone and Tintoretto, Veronese felt drawn to the decorative side of Titian's art, and, like Titian, he covered a wide range of subject matter including portraits.

In Veronese's creations, figures from Christian lore and portraits of his friends peacefully coexisted. The painter found it perfectly normal to idealise secular contemporaries such as senators and courtiers into sacred personages–a way to reconcile man with his past. He perceived reality without preconceived ideas; in his vast decorative compositions, an unchallenged handling of colour and an unequalled mastery of perspectival devices rendered his art inappropriate for intellectual concepts, either philosophical or religious. It was suitable for displaying reality in its most brilliant and charming aspect. Carlo Ridolfi, a seventeenth-century art historian wrote: "He favoured joy and made beauty stately and laughter gay."[1]

This new variation of humanism would transform the widespread inspiration of universal tolerance into images. Veronese's ability to bring the joys of life into Venetian homes with his scenes of sumptuous feasts in a superb decor of arcades, pillars, and staircases–all aglitter with gold, precious stones, silks and brocades in enchanting silvery colour schemes, highlighted by a sudden sparkle of brilliant greens, vermilion, and resplendent yellows–show him to be an intuitive painter of impressionistic tendencies. He truly personified the profound movement of pictorial creativity that made the city one of the most unusual centres of the times.

Venice had done her utmost to occupy a permanent spot in history holding the same rank–in spite of her recent birth–as the most prestigious cities of the world. Furthermore, the exact path that Venice followed shows that she never imitated, copied, or reproduced what she could discover elsewhere. She had known how to accumulate and attract, like a magnet, that which best served her glory. She thus appropriated loot from Constantinople, from Egypt, and Greece, as well as from Rome and Florence. Venice exercised an influence that enhanced the talent of those who chose to settle and work there. This was the case for Verrocchio, for example, when he

1. Carlo Ridolfi, *Le maraviglie dell'Arte*, Venice, 1648.

executed his superb statue of Colleoni at the end of the fifteenth century. The same remark can be made with regard to Antonello da Messina who painted the *Portrait of a Condottiere* in the same period.

During the most fleeting moments of her triumph, Venice inspired those who loved her. To this, Veronese bears testimony more than any other painter. It is thus in Venice, whose triumph he never ceased to celebrate, that his works should be seen. The most famous of his creations *The Marriage at Cana* (1562-1563, Louvre), however, has been in Paris since 1798.

Left, preceding pages and following pages

VERONESE
The Marriage at Cana
details
see p. 168

FREEDOM FOR POETS AND JESTERS

"We painters take the same license as poets and jesters and I represented the two halberdiers–one drinking, the other eating–at the foot of the stairs, but both ready to do their duty, because it seemed to me fitting and probable that the master of the house, whom I was told was rich and magnificent, should have such servants...."[1]

This was Veronese's explanation when he faced the tribune of the most severe Inquisitors and was ordered to justify his over-personal interpretation of *The Last Supper* (commissioned for the Convent of SS. Giovanni e Paolo to replace the one painted by Titian which had just been destroyed in a fire).

The painter's energetic reaction in front of his judges demonstrates both his susceptibility and his irony; but perhaps his words could also be interpreted as profoundly sincere. To affirm loud and clear that the numinous is better expressed by genuine feelings than by a pedestrian respect for convention is a point of view that deserves consideration. Veronese proclaimed that genuineness in expressing feelings, indeed, transcends mythology, history and the uncertainty of the present, allowing a painting to be used as 'a pretext for colour.' This is how *The Marriage at Cana* should be appreciated. More than an illustration of a scene from the New Testament, it is a hymn to a colourful celebration in a Venetian palace. And what a gathering!

In the foreground, the artist is accompanying a group of distinguished colleagues in an instrumental ensemble of chamber music: Titian, in red, is keeping the tempo on a double-bass; Tintoretto is playing the viola; Jacopo Bassano is blowing into a flute, and Veronese himself, in yellow, is playing on a violoncello. The painters–not only music lovers but excellent musicians–honour their hosts while animating the banquet. They give the occasion a profane as well as a religious meaningfulness. We should bear in mind that the theme, frequently used since the Middle Ages to decorate refectories, is one of a wedding. The Evangelist St. John thus narrates the first miracle of Christ:

1 Pietro Caliari, *Paolo Veronese*, Rome, 1888.

"Two days later there was a wedding in the town of Cana in Galilee. Jesus' mother was there and Jesus and his disciples had also been invited to the wedding. When the wine had given out, Jesus' mother said to him, 'They have no wine left.'

Jesus replied. 'You must not tell me what to do, my time has not yet come.'

Jesus' mother then told the servants, 'Do whatever He tells you.'

The Jews have rules about ritual washing, and for this purpose six stone water jars were there, each one large enough to hold about a hundred litres.

Jesus said to the servants, 'Fill these jars with water.' They filled them to the brim, and then He told them, 'Now draw some water off and take it to the steward of the feast.'

The steward tasted the water now turned into wine, not knowing its source; though the servants who had drawn out the water knew; so the steward called the bridegroom and said to him, 'Everyone else serves the best wine first, and after the guests have had plenty to drink, he serves the ordinary wine. But you have kept the best wine until now!'

Jesus performed this first miracle in Cana in Galilee, where He revealed his glory, and his disciples believed in him."

In 1562, the restructuring of the refectory was finished. It was built like an optical system focusing all the light on the wall where Veronese's work would be hung. It seems that long before the final contract was signed, the two artists had reached an agreement on the execution of the whole project. They would repeat at S. Giorgio what they had so splendidly succeeded at Maser for the Barbaro family and in just as superb a manner, for the glory of the Benedictines but also for the glory of Venice.

A SPECTACULAR SYMMETRY

When Veronese began to paint–*in situ*–the gigantic composition that he would finish the following year, the theme had just been treated in 1561 by Tintoretto (see chapter *A Child of Venice)*, for another refectory at the Monastery of the Padri Crociferi. The work can been seen today at Church of S. Maria della Salute.

Veronese decided to do the exact opposite of Tintoretto. Where Tintoretto created an asymmetrical space with extreme tension, Veronese based his composition on a spectacular symmetry. Christ, motionless, is the central point around which the figures are regrouped in three juxtaposed circles. The vertical axis passing through the middle of Jesus' body separates the bottom half of the canvas into two symbolically equal parts: the princes on the left, the disciples and the clerics on the right.

The guests and the servants are scattered around the middle of the composition: the Good News can be shared by everyone, no matter what his role or his position. The upper half of the canvas, dominated by the azure sky, is divided by a balustrade forming a horizontal axis; the bottom half, decorated with the pink marble of Verona, contains the principal figures of the scene.

Undoubtedly, this is a theatre performance putting on the miracle. And the show is taking place, not as it was for Tintoretto's version in an inn, but in a sumptuous Venetian palace set on a stage conceived by Palladio, and we are invited to the wedding breakfast. Three basic subjects are expressed in this grandiose spectacle: the wedding breakfast which is the central pretext for the painting, the architecture which comprises the decor, and the music that subtly enhances the scene's magnificence.

THE BANQUET

When Veronese decided to take on this project, he was inspired by sources other than merely the Scriptures of the New Testament. He had become immersed in a recent literary description of the miracle by his friend Aretino. In addition to his talent as chronicler of political and artistic news, Aretino was the author of a book published in 1539, *I Quattro Libri del'Humanità di Christo*, in which, by taking some liberties with the Gospel, he had situated the episode of the Miracle at Cana in a luxurious setting. He described a royal feast, putting emphasis on the splendour of the couple's clothing. The scene took place at court and therefore it was normal that, in addition to secular and religious dignitaries, professional musicians performed during the festivities. It was also traditional for the meal to be exceptionally sumptuous; gold vases, carved silver dishes, sculpted armchairs, and the most delicious food was present on the table. Charles Diehl draws our attention to the many splendours of a Venetian feast and describes a banquet in detail:

"On the tables, covered with finely embroidered cloths, the silver and gold candelabra sparkled next to the enamelled bowls, silver fountains, centrepieces filled with sweetmeats or with aromatic herbs. The side tables placed around the hall exposed rare pieces of majolica, precious plates, and glasses with deliciously complicated shapes. The napkins were folded into turbans or mitres, crowns or pyramids. The scent of perfume floated in the air. Flowers placed in front of each guest added to the luxurious harmony. Above all, the menu was extraordinary: oysters and truffles, salads and sausages, hams, hors-d'œuvres, twenty different pottages, sturgeon from Ferrara, eels from Binasco, sausage from Modena, tripes from Trevisa, thrushes from Perugia, quail from Lombardy, geese from Romagna, pasta from Genoa; pastry and all kinds of fruit were carried in

Left, above, and following pages

VERONESE (PAOLO CALIARI, C. 1530-1588)
The Marriage at Cana
1562-1563, canvas, 22 x 32$^{1}/_{2}$ ft.
(666 x 990 cm)
Paris, musée du Louvre

This picture hung in the Refectory of the Benedictine Monastery of S. Giorgio Maggiore until it was taken to Paris after the downfall of the *Serenissima* in 1797.

and sometimes accompanied with strange seasonings, not to mention the spices that were used; sugar was added to roasts and fish, and sometimes perfumed water to the sauces. A variety of wines completed this gastronomic spread: muscatel from Candia and malmsey from Cyprus, as well as Hungarian and Rhine wines."[1]

Had Aretino intended to make a stronger contrast with the humility of Christ by exaggerating the atmosphere of opulence? Did he feel that it would better justify the moralising nature of Christ to have this wedding breakfast such a lavish occasion? The only part of the Scriptures that Aretino followed scrupulously was the moment when the wine ran out. When the meal reached the dessert course, he described the miracle that the painter would glorify in his illustration of Aretino's text:

"'Pour a glass and carry it to the wine taster.' The servants poured and carried it to the sommelier who, when he smelled the wine and discovered that it had come from celestial vines, recovered his spirits [...] At the first sip he felt a sweet tingling right down to his toes. When he had finished a glassful, he claimed that it had been filled with distilled rubies."

Aretino described and Veronese painted this moment in a delicate manner.

INSPIRING ARCHITECTURE

Above the balustrade on each side of the painting, an ensemble of symmetrical pillars frames the scene which is taking place in a princely palace, emphasising the theatrical effect. In his picture, Veronese freely handled the painted scenery. Through the magic of trompe-l'œil, he produced a fascinating composition by juxtaposing different architectural elements, some designed to decorate interior spaces, others to fit the outside of buildings. Such an exceptional homogeneous spatial effect reminds us of the marvellous architectural intuition of Sansovino and Palladio in achieving a graceful fluidity between the inside and the outside of their buildings. Here, the miracle of the transformation of water into wine is associated with the magic of this metaphysical dream, where the distinction between what is here (reality) and what is elsewhere (reverie) has been abolished. Reality and reverie flow one into the other, reconciled into a superior harmony by art.

What seemed to have interested Veronese regarding Sansovino was the successful association that the architect produced with the different coloured materials and sculpted elements, in particular with his Loggetta: statues, columns, etc. From Palladio, Veronese learned the visual articulation of forms in space that the Vicentine obtained through his various uses of columns. Veronese found a way to render homage to his

1. C. Diehl, *op. cit.*

inspirers by making visual quotations of their architectural works at the top of the canvas, in direct relation to the sky where only birds and geniuses have their place.

MUSIC AND PAINTERS

No Venetian banquet took place that was not animated by jesters and musicians. It does not really matter that Veronese has been thought to have placed the group of musicians in the foreground of his *Marriage at Cana* simply to paint portraits of his friends. What is important is the part held by music in Venice and nothing could have been more commonplace in a city where public life was rhythmed by celebrations and other festivities; these would have been dull if music had not accompanied them.

The same tradition was widespread in the milieu of painters. All witnesses confirm that Giorgione, Tintoretto and Titian were excellent instrumentalists. Vasari mentioned that Giorgione played the lute so well that patricians often summoned him to their palaces for concerts. Tintoretto, a friend of the composer Zarlino, took "pleasure in cultivating all the arts and in particular music," which was known to stimulate his prodigious creativity. We know that Titian exchanged with the instrument maker Trasuntino one of his paintings for a portable organ, around 1540. It could be the one that is depicted in his superb *Venus and the Organ Player with an Amoretto.*

Since no banquet worthy of its name could take place without music, it is clear that a painter who wished to evoke the charms of such an event could not leave musicians out of his painting. It was his manner of adding a silent rhythm and finishing touches to emotions. When we consider the number of paintings which, until the end of the nineteenth century, were to be inspired by *The Marriage at Cana* (not counting the many copies executed), we observe that none of these has left out the musicians.

The Marriage at Cana is thus an immense social event. Facing the Benedictine fathers on the right side of the canvas–in deference to patronage–and next to the newly-weds are the socialites in varied costumes, both Europeans and oriental. The work literally swarms with picturesque details that give a familiar and secular tone to the whole, without in any way altering the extravagance such as the dogs on the table, on the lap of the bridegroom, and at the foot of the musicians. Other examples are the cat who is sharpening its claws on a keg, the dwarf feeding his parrot, and the steward who–like an actor of the Commedia dell' Arte–addresses the couple: "Everyone else serves the best wine first, and after the guests have had plenty to drink, he serves the ordinary wine. But you have kept the best wine until now!"

The way that Veronese designed costumes and sets, controlled actors' gestures and attitudes, blocked stage movements for a crowd of one hundred and thirty people engaged in diverse activities–as a theatre director would–turned the painting into a successful performance. The painter's art is an art of dramatic composition.

VERONESE
The Marriage at Cana
1571, canvas, 7 x 15 ft. (207 x 457 cm)
Dresden, Staatliche Kunstsammlungen,
Galerie Alte Meister

DRESDEN'S MARRIAGE AT CANA

Several years later at the request of the Cuccina family, Veronese undertook another version of the same theme. This canvas has more modest dimensions. Conserved at the Dresden Museum, it is the antithesis of the one painted for S. Giorgio Maggiore. It is the wine taster, often taken for a self-portrait of Veronese, who visually constitutes the central figure and who, with an extremely elegant gesture, invites us to share the miracle of excellence. Here, we are further removed from an evangelistic message, but closer to Venice's unrestrained love of the celebration of pleasure.

REFLECTIONS OF VENICE

CANALETTO, GUARDI, CANOVA AND OTHERS

Amusingly enough, the architect who had the privilege of building the Rialto Bridge (*ponte* in Italian) was called Antonio Da Ponte and the name of one of the most famous *vedutisti* painters was Antonio Canal. 'Il Canaletto' was born in Venice, near the Grand Canal, on October 28, 1697.

A bitter rivalry had opposed the Canale and Da Ponte families for several generations; they had not ceased to confront each other at all occasions, in the Senate and elsewhere. Venice escaped her downfall, within a hair's breath, over this dispute. One day during a parliamentary session, a Da Ponte exclaimed to his adversary Canale, "The bridges are above the canals!" And the latter answered, "Without the canals, the bridges wouldn't exist." The exasperated Doge ordered them to stop their endless squabbling. He then went as far as threatening to demolish literally both their arguments; in other words, he would topple the bridges and fill in the canals. We do not know if this menace was enough to put a stop to the quarrel that Dada would try to re-engage at the beginning of the twentieth century. The important fact is that the canals and the bridges still exist today.

Pietro Longhi (1702-1785)
Il Ridotto
c. 1757, canvas, 24 x 19 1/4 in.
(61 x 49 cm)
Venice, Fondazione Querini-Stampalia

CANALETTO'S THEATRE: THE VEDUTE

CANALETTO (ANTONIO CANAL, 1697-1768)
The Piazza in front of the Church of John and Paul
c. 1725, canvas, 49 1/4 x 65 in.
(125 x 165 cm)
Dresden, Galerie Alte Meister

It was while working with his father, a painter of theatrical scenery of great renown, that the young assistant discovered the beautiful stage sets in fashion in Venice at the time. The sets of the exterior scenes were arranged with trees, arbours, and statues and designed in perspective; the height of the stage was such that the actors and singers seemed minute, like the figures which would appear later in Canaletto's paintings. Perspective reigned and helped solve one of the most intricate problems that challenged set designers: how to represent on the stage an interior with a corner made of pillars, porticoes, and balustrades. The architectural devices that Veronese had included in his paintings, the father and son now put on stage.

While the artist began working on the sets of Vivaldi's two opera houses, he rubbed shoulders with the theatre crowd–a world high with colour, tumult, fantasy, frivolity, and resourcefulness. He may have met musicians such as Monteverdi and Carissimi, famous throughout Europe, and the sublime young ladies from the religious institutions who 'sang like angels' and went by the enchanting names of Pierina del Violino, Cattarina del Cornetto, Bettina della Viola, Claudia del Flautino. He began to represent the different people that he could observe while working at the theatres.

At the age of twenty two, Canaletto accompanied his father to Rome where they executed two sets for Scarlatti operas. It was during one of these trips that the young painter became aware of his talent and his ambition. He decided to revolutionise the art of the *vedutà*. He then became the 'portraitist' of his native city. Careful observation of his views of Venice, his genre scenes, and his *capricci*–fanciful landscapes with imaginary architecture as opposed to his *vedute* which depicted actual locations–shows that they were indeed all composed according to the principles of theatre staging. Canaletto learned many visual devices from the theatre such as how to link together an assortment of themes into a unified composition; he knew how to distribute contrasting masses of light and dark, cast shadows across the scenes, or plunge the foreground into deep shade in order to create an impression of depth. His figures are almost always seen from behind–the opposite of a portrait; they play the essential role of conducting the eye of the viewer towards the decor.

Very quickly Canaletto made a name for himself in a genre that would become very popular with foreign collectors, in particular with the English. This was a period when benefactors changed their habits. A patron could no longer simply put together a personal collection exclusively for his own pleasure. The emerging concept of the art gallery in the eighteenth century has been discussed by art historians such as Francis Haskell, who explained that this transformation took place under the

Right and following pages

CANALETTO
The Grand Canal, Looking Northeast Towards the Rialto Bridge
1726-1730, canvas, $57^{1/2}$ x $98^{1/8}$ in. (146 x 234 cm)
Dresden, Staatliche Kunstsammlungen, Galerie Alte Meister

influence of Francesco Algarotti. Critic and patron in his own right, Algarotti, "in Dresden,[...] drew up a plan for extending and completing the spectacular art gallery which was being formed by Augustus of Saxony."[1]

Canaletto spared no effort in scattering his pictures of Venice's bridges and canals throughout Europe. A new approach to art dealing was developing, inspired directly by the commercial methods of buying and selling perishables. In 1729, when Joseph Smith met Canaletto, the Englishman was registered in Venice as an agent importing meats and fish–not necessarily

1. Francis Haskell, *Patrons and Painters*, London, 1963.

incompatible with an interest in art. He collected paintings and rare books and held a salon in his palace on the Grand Canal, near the Church of the SS. Apostoli. For many years, Canaletto would continue to paint a very important series of *vedute* and *capricci* for Smith who later sold them to George III, the King of England.

The largest part of Canaletto's artistic production, therefore, left Venice for England where Smith had introduced the painter to high society. When in 1744, in gratitude for the services he had rendered, Smith was appointed consul of his Gracious Majesty, the King of England to the *Serenissima*, his fortune was made. He owned thirty-eight paintings by

CANALETTO
Rio dei Mendicanti, Looking South
c. 1740, canvas, 56 1/4 x 78 3/4 in.
(143 x 200 cm)
Venice, Ca' Rezzonico

Canaletto; the collections of the Duke of Buckingham and Count Carlysle were also well stocked–twenty belonged to the Duke and fifteen to the Count.

ATMOSPHERIC CONTRAST

Then Canaletto decided to settle in London and was immediately drawn into a veritable marathon of painting. His clients were of such high rank and in such a hurry that he could hardly find the time to satisfy their demands. But, in spite of the energy that he spent, Canaletto was not able to convince the English art-lover that London could not be bathed in the ethereal light so typical of Venice. He was criticized for exaggerating perspectives and accused of over-using the camera obscura *(ottica)*. After nearly ten years in London, Canaletto returned to Venice. He wanted to rediscover 'his' light, and observe a less hectic schedule.

In 1763, after one unsuccessful attempt, he was admitted to the Accademia. Although considering that *vedute* did not constitute a 'noble and edifying' genre, the members of the institution allowed him to join. Following the tradition, Canaletto offered a perspective fantasy to the Accademia–one of the few works of his that is still in Venice today.

THE VEDUTE: THE ENLARGEMENT OF PHOTOGRAPHIC SPACE

Canaletto heralded Venice's infatuation with herself. There was no show of smugness in his work, for he manifested great reverence towards his native city. Nothing of her past nor her glory was unknown to him, yet he seemed to perceive the ephemerality of Venice. Although still queen of the sea, still the most serene of republics, she was on the verge of collapse.

When Canaletto decided to carry on the tradition of the *vedute* launched by Carlevaris and Ricci, he renovated the technique in order to capture a natural light in his paintings. He also enlarged the angles of vision and multiplied the perspectives, thus adding space and escaping from photographic realism.

While painting from life, he may have drawn sketches with the help of an *ottico*–an improved version of the camera obscura employed by some painters of the previous century such as Vermeer. He may have found this ancestor of the photographic camera useful when working on the composition of a painting. He knew, however, that he would have to correct the perspective and the tones produced by the camera. In any case if he had utilised such an optical device, he would have translated the raw information given by the instrument into delicate atmospheric gradations.

Furthermore, Canaletto remarkably depicted Venice as she was and how she saw herself in the middle of the eighteenth century–a city that, for want of being invincible, had become inimitable. She had no reason to be ashamed of the way Canaletto caught her reflection in the waters of the canals.

CANALETTO
The Molo, Seen from St. Mark's Basin
canvas, 18 1/2 x 31 7/8 in.
(47 x 81 cm)
Paris, musée du Louvre

Francesco Guardi (1712-1793)
The Procession of the Doge in front of S. Zaccaria on Easter Day
c. 1766-1770, canvas, 26 x 39 3/4 in. (66 x 101 cm)
Paris, musée du Louvre

GUARDI AND ROMANTICISM

Pietro Longhi
Portrait of Francesco Guardi
canvas, 52 x $39^{3}/8$ in. (132 x 100 cm)
Venice, Ca' Rezzonico

Francesco Guardi discovered the soul of Venice in her light and air; he felt it in the endless nuances and in the changing variations of her waters and her sky with a quivering swift and spontaneous touch of modern impressionism. For him, nothing was the fruit of improvisation. The quality of his preparatory drawings demonstrates that the tension found in his compositions is intentional; a strict structure is hidden under the vibration of colours and forms. "The sparkling light and quick broken-up touches of colour create a lyric atmosphere that suggests a pre-romantic nostalgia."[1] Fifteen years younger than Canaletto, Guardi was the first of the Venetian romantics.

Unlike the Canaletto lineage, the Guardi painters were not originally from Venice but from Mastellina in the Val di Sole (Trentino region). Francesco Guardi, however, was born in Venice in 1712 and appropriated Canaletto's place, left vacant by the decision of the latter to settle in London. Everything set Guardi apart from his illustrious predecessor–first of all, his approach to light. Guardi created a shimmering ambience in truly lyrical surroundings. The urban landscape was no longer the subject treated, even as a decor; it became the expression of genuine feelings. Guardi's Venice, no longer a reflection of herself, had become an image projected by the beliefs and emotions of the painter. The unique theme of his work was an eighteenth-century city falling into decadence. When Guardi blurred the outlines of the monuments into magical chiaroscuro and when he made the water and the reflections of the palaces tremble with uneasy touches, he was interpreting the transience of human endeavour.

Ever since Giorgione's *Tempesta*, we have been able to observe the sharp sense of tragedy with which Venetian painting was imbued. In Titian's later works, tragedy was transformed into foreboding. Canaletto and Guardi led us into an illusory universe. To the first, the world became a theatre; to the second even illusion was specious, for nothing could interrupt the approaching decline.

Crumbling facades baked by the sun and the salt, canals obstructed by barques, gondolas with torn canopies, this artistic use of contemporary everyday material in preference to the legendary, mythological, or historical images, barely contradicted the paintings of the great ceremonies and feasts presided over by the Doge. These festive occasions did not, however, turn to parody, for they continued to be held with a deep respect to tradition. Mist enveloped the Riva degli Schiavoni and, in the distance, the Doge's Palace and St. Mark's Basin evaporated into the haze. The *Bucentoro* continued to glide along the lagoon because this was the role

1. A. Chastel, in Mary McCarthy, *Venice Observed*, Paris 1956.

Francesco Guardi
The Nun's Parlor
canvas, 45 x 80 7/8 in. (114.3 x 205.4 cm)
Venice, Ca' Rezzonico

This painting is the companion-piece to *Il Ridotto (The Gaming Room)*.

PIETRO LONGHI
The Rhinoceros
c. 1751, canvas, $24^{3}/8 \times 19^{3}/4$ in.
(62 x 50 cm)
Venice, Ca' Rezzonico

Venice's carnival offered countless festivities… for the idle bourgeois!

that Venice assumed, but the fervour had died and the folly had faded. In all the paintings of ceremonies, luxury gave its seat to boredom. The triumphant seafarers and ambitious merchants had become mere figureheads. They no longer played the roles that their offices evoked; they had become mere actors. In other scenes such as the *Procession at S. Zacharia* (1766-1770, Louvre), a procession of phantoms enters the church.

Francesco Guardi died on January l, 1793 before Doge Ludovico Manin abandoned the Ducal Palace on May 12, 1797 and left authority in the hands of the French. Guardi neither lived to see the treaty of Campo Formio, nor *The Marriage at Cana* leave for Paris, nor the end of a thousand years of commercial, military, and artistic endeavour. His last wish may have been that all which Venice had reaped, amassed and created would provide her with immortality.

Opposite

Giandomenico Tiepolo (1727-1804)
The Tooth Puller
detail
c. 1754, canvas, 31 3/4 x 43 1/4 in.
(80.5 x 110 cm)
Paris, musée du Louvre

Right

Giandomenico Tiepolo
The Carnival Scene or the Minuet
detail
c. 1754-1755, canvas, 31 3/4 x 43 1/2 in.
(80.5 x 110.5 cm)
Paris, musée du Louvre

GIANDOMENICO TIEPOLO (1727-1804)
The New World
1791, detached fresco
from the Villa Tiepolo,
7 x 17 ft. (205 x 525 cm)
Venice, Ca' Rezzonico

A crowd of idlers gather to watch a *cosmorama*.

Right

GIANDOMENICO TIEPOLO
Buffoons and Acrobats
1793, detached fresco
from the Villa Tiepolo,
100 x 55 in. (196 x 160 cm)
Venice, Ca' Rezzonico

THE SENSUALITY OF CANOVA

Thank heavens, Venice died hard! She remembered the celebrations that she had given. She awoke each year for her carnival (Pietro Longhi). She had fun (Tiepolo). She stood aloof from herself. Having rid herself of illusions, she had also lost hope. This did not mean that she was about to fall into despair. Even if her joy was less sincere, today's merriment might help her forget her exuberant past in which Venetian art had found the sources of its creativity and the resources of its innovations. Now, Venice took inspiration from what was being accomplished elsewhere in Europe.

This is what the sculptor Antonio Canova (1757-1822) did in the second half of the eighteenth century. He took leave of the Baroque language that had flowered in seventeenth-century Venice and opened the chapter of Neo-Classicism, becoming one of its greatest representatives. After his artistic debut on the banks of the Grand Canal, the neo-classical sculptor executed almost all of his works in the heart of Rome–no man is a prophet in his own country! His country had spread to Europe, into which he had fused. Venice was no longer contained in Venice.

Full of grace and sensuality, the beautiful marble on show at the Louvre, *Psyche Revived by Cupid's Kiss* (1787-1793), was one of Canova's most successful pieces. The sculptor was thought to have been the lover of Princess Pauline Borghese, sister of Napoleon I. His rendition of her as a reclining Venus enchanted her husband, but no one else had a chance to judge it. The prince, who certainly was not jealous of his wife, was jealous of her statue. He kept it locked up in a room in the Borghese Palace, of which he held the key and no one, not even Canova himself, could get access to the room. The piece shows the artist's taste for polished marble that led him to soften the forms and give more importance to line; it was no longer the volumes that counted but the elegance of the well-delineated contours. Sculpture thus became a meditation on grace. Venice was now prepared to welcome the romantic traveller filled with wonder, in quest of his own image and, who knows, his identity.

Above

ANTONIO CANOVA (1757-1822)
Pauline Bonaparte Borghese as Venus Victorious
1804-1808, polychrome marble
Rome, Galleria Borghese

Left

ANTONIO CANOVA
Psyche Revived by Cupid's Kiss
detail
1787-1793, marble,
61 x 66 1/8 in. (155 x 168 cm)
Paris, musée du Louvre

ANTONIO CANOVA
Cupid and Psyche
1796-1800, marble, 59 1/8 in. (150 cm)
Paris, musée du Louvre

Right

ANTONIO CANOVA
Cupid and Psyche
detail
plaster
Possagno, Gipsoteca

The plaster cast prepared for the pointing process before being cut into marble.

VENICE AFTER VENICE

Tintoretto with his *Crucifixion* prefigured the cinematographer. Canaletto with his *vedute* prefigured the postcard. Everything was prepared to welcome the travellers who wander around in droves, in a city which created herself for them over a period of a thousand years. "The most triumphant city that I have ever seen… governed with the greatest wisdom and serving God with the greatest solemnity." exclaimed Philippe de Commynes in 1494. Five hundred years later, her glorious image remains, as remains the jubilation.

In Michel Butor's words: "The flow of the crowd is as indispensable to the facade of St. Mark's as the flow of the canals to the palaces. So many ancient monuments have been diverted from their true function by the tourists who flock there, that we have the impression that the buildings are being desecrated, even by ourselves, of course, when we visit them outside the framework of scholarship. These private, secret, closed, forbidden, gutted, and silent places for contemplation are spoiled by chattering. The Basilica, with the city surrounding it, has nothing to fear from this fauna and our own trivia; it was born and has endured under the constant gaze of visitors and artists who worked among the conversations of seamen and merchants."

For Jean Paul Sartre: "In Venice, nothing is simple, because it isn't a city. No, it's an archipelago. How could we forget this? From your island, you look out at the island opposite with envy; over there, what is there?–solitude, purity and silence that are not, you well know, on this side. The true Venice, no matter where you are, will always be elsewhere."

Is it her coquettish talent for attracting attention and admiration, yet permitting no more than elusive encounters, that allows Venice to keep alive the memory of her enigmatic birth, evasive past, contradictory present, uncertain future, and thus postpone her death?

The Church of S. Giorgio Maggiore
Venice

Seen from the room that George Sand and Alfred de Musset occupied at the Hotel Danieli.

FURTHER

Vittore Carpaccio
The Legend of St. Ursula
The Engaged Couple Taking Leave of their Parents
detail
see p. 85

ARETINO, Pietro, *Selected Letters,* trans. by George Bull, London, Penguin Classics, 1976.

BERENSON, Bernard, *Italian Pictures of the Renaissance. Venetian Schools,* 2 vol., London, 1957.

BRAUDEL, Fernand, *Out of Italy, 1450-1650,* trans. by Sian Reyno, Paris, Flammarion, 1991.

BRODSKY, Joseph, *Watermark,* New York, Farrar, Strauss & Giroux, 1992.

BUTOR, Michel, *Description de Saint-Marc,* Paris, Gallimard, 1963.

CHASTEL, André, *L'art italien,* Paris, Flammarion, 1982

DIEHL C., *Venise, une République patricienne,* Paris, 1928 (reprinted in 1985 by Flammarion under the title: *La République de Venise).*

FAURE, Elie, *History of Art,* Garden City Publishing, 1937.

FRANCASTEL, Pierre, *Peinture et société,* Paris, Denoël, 1952.

GOETHE, Johann Wolgang von, *Viaggio in Italia,* a cura di A. Farinelli (1740), Roma 1932.

HALE, John R., *Encyclopedia of the Italian Renaissance,* London, Thames & Hudson, 1981.

HASKELL, Francis, *Patrons and Painters, Art and Society in Baroque Italy,* New York, Alfred A. Knopf, 1963.

LANE, F. C., *Venice: A Maritime Republic,* London, 1973.

LAUTS, J., *Carpaccio,* London, 1962.

MARTINEAU, Jane & HOPE, Charles, editors, *The Genius of Venice, 1500-1600,* Catalogue of an exhibition at the Royal Academy of Arts, London, Weidenfeld & Nicolson, 1983.

READING

McCARTHY, Mary, *Venice Observed,* with comments by André Chastel, Lausanne, 1956.

MORRIS, James, *Venice,* London, Faber & Faber, 1960.

MUSÉE DU LOUVRE, *Les Noces de Cana de Véronèse : une œuvre et sa restauration,* Paris, 1993.

NEUMANN, Jaromis, *Titian: The Flaying of Marsyas,* London, 1965.

PALLADIO, Andrea, *Architecture of Palladio in Four Books,* trans. by Giacomo Leoni, London, 1715.

PANOFSKY, Erwin, *Problems in Titian, Mostly Iconographic,* New York, 1969.

PIGNATTI, Terisio, *Pittura Veneziana del Cinquecento,* Bergamo, 1947.

POLO, Marco, *The Travels,* Harmondsworth, Penguin, 1958.

RIDOLFI, Carlo, *Le maraviglie dell'Arte,* Venice, 1648.

RILKE, Rainer Maria, *Gesammelte Werke,* Leipzig, 1927.

ROSKILL, Mark W., *Dolce's Aretino and Venetian Art, Theory of the Cinquecento,* New York, 1968.

RUSKIN, John, *The Stones of Venice,* London, 1951.

SARTRE, Jean-Paul, *Situations IV,* Paris, Gallimard, 1964.

STENDHAL, *Chroniques italiennes,* Paris, Gallimard, 1986

TIETZE, Hans, *Tintoretto. The Paintings and Drawings,* London, Phaidon, 1948.

TIETZE, Hans, *Titian. The Paintings and Drawings,* London, Phaidon, 1950.

VASARI, Giorgio, *Lives of the Painters, Sculptors, and Architects,* 4 vols., London, Everyman's Library, 1927.

WILDE, J., *Venetian Art from Bellini to Titian,* Oxford, 1974.

WIND, Edgar, *Giorgione's Tempesta,* Oxford, 1969.

Vittore Carpaccio
Two Courtesans
wood, 37 x 25 1/4 in. (94 x 64 cm)
Venice, Museo Correr

Left

Gentile Bellini
**Gianfrancesco II Gonzaga,
Comte de Mantua**
wood, 25 3/8 x 18 7/8 in. (62 x 48 cm)
Bergamo, Accademia Carrara

Printed in Italy